THE COMPLETE BOOK OF WEEKEND GARDEN PROJECTS

THE COMPLETE
BOOK OF WEEKEND
GARDEN PROJECTS

COMPILED AND EDITED BY JENNY HENDY

PUBLISHED BY
SALAMANDER BOOKS LIMITED
LONDON

This edition published in 2001 by
Salamander Books Ltd.,
8, Blenheim Court, Brewery Road,
London N7 9NY, United Kingdom

A member of the Chrysalis Group plc

© 2001 Salamander Books Limited

ISBN 1 84065 282 9
Printed and bound in Taiwan

credits

Compiler and consultant editor: Jenny Hendy
Designed and edited by: FOCUS PUBLISHING,
The Courtyard, 26 London Road, Sevenoaks,
Kent TN13 1AP
Project editor: Guy Croton
Designer: Philip Clucas MSIAD
Project coordinator: David Etherington
Picture researcher: Caroline Watson
Photographer: Neil Sutherland
Salamander editorial director: Will Steeds
Salamander production: Phillip Chamberlain
Salamander art director: John Heritage

about the author

Jenny Hendy's love affair with plants and gardens
began very early on. She gained an honours degree
in botany at U.C.N.W. Bangor, taking a job in a
garden centre following graduation. In 1985 she
joined the staff of *Gardening from Which?* magazine
and began producing articles. A freelance writer
for the last ten years, she has authored and
contributed to many titles as well as appearing
on television. In addition to writing, she now
runs her own garden design consultancy.

CONTENTS

Foreword

The irony of my situation is that I spend far more time writing about gardening and helping other people to create gardens than I do actually gardening on my own, so I know how frustrating it can be when work gets in the way. But one way or another I usually manage to sneak in a few hours here and there. Some of us love to garden for the sake of it, revelling in the contact with nature, whilst others simply want an attractive place to look out onto and are quite happy to pay for other people to do the work. In compiling this book I hope I have gone some way towards bridging the gap between these two extremes and perhaps to persuade people who have never gardened to try it out. You may have little or no gardening or DIY experience, but don't let that put you off. You will be amazed at what you can achieve by yourself and friends and family are often more than happy to help out should the need arise.

No matter what your level of experience, I would encourage you to visit gardens and flower shows and to make a mental note of the plants and features that you want to incorporate into your own garden. Magazines, books and TV programmes can also be a valuable source of inspiration. Fashions and trends come and go whether you are decorating an interior or exterior space, but the important thing is to do what feels right for you and to create an environment that suits your personality. Gardens are places for self-expression and are very accommodating. Speaking decoratively, in some ways you can be far more adventurous in your garden room and if something is not perfect that often adds to the relaxed atmosphere.

If yours is an established garden, you may feel that there is little more you can do to improve it. But one of the challenges for more experienced gardeners in this situation is to recognise that gardens are dynamic, not static places. Plants grow, altering the perspective, materials weather and the passage of the seasons cause an infinite number of subtle changes to occur. Ask yourself what you like and dislike about your garden and what you want to do differently and then use this book to turn your ideas into reality.

Jenny Hendy

left: *There are few things more pleasing to the eye than a well planned and established garden with all elements working together in harmony.*

Introduction

above: *Wood is a lovely material to work with and this book includes several straightforward projects for you to incorporate into your garden.*

Few of us these days are able to devote much time to the garden and the weekend is often the only chance we have to get out there. This book is designed to provide a series of mini projects that in the main can be tackled within those two days. In addition to the projects there is plenty of practical advice on how to make gardening less of a chore and more of a pleasure, as well as inspirational design ideas showing a wealth of decorating possibilities for your outdoor room.

When you are limited to just a few hours leisure time but still want to get things done, the secret to success is organisation. That is why the practical sections in this book all contain a checklist of items that you need as well as a rough idea of how long the project is likely to take. Gathering all your tools and 'ingredients' together at the start of a project will save those frantic last minute dashes to the garden centre or DIY store and allow you to enjoy what you are doing and be more relaxed about it. After all, gardening should be fun and can be a very rewarding and stimulating activity.

No matter what stage you have reached with your garden, you will find lots of ideas and information to help within the following pages. You may have just moved in to a place and have a garden to create from scratch or one to renovate and develop. Alternatively, you may have gardened the same plot for years. When you have lived in a place for quite a period, the garden can often go through the doldrums, neglected through lack of time, energy and inspiration. This book will encourage you to give the garden a makeover and inject some new life into it, as you thoroughly shake out the cobwebs!

Some of the projects require a little more DIY or gardening know-how than average, but the vast majority can be tackled by beginners in both camps; just follow the simple step-by-step instructions. And if you do need further advice or reassurance, ask at your local garden centre or DIY store. Their staff are often only too willing to help and can take some of

above: *Gather key ingredients together to save time and make any task that much easier. Grouping plants beforehand helps you design your arrangement.*

the stress out of making decisions such as what power of submersible pump you need for a water feature or how much gravel to order for a patio. Try to find out as much as possible about your garden and the local conditions before embarking on any major planting projects. This will save you from making expensive mistakes such as buying plants that are too tender to survive the winter in your area.

The first part of the book contains a series of styling suggestions including how to create the cottage garden look or a feeling of classical grandeur, and there are shorthand design notes outlining the key elements that make a particular theme distinctive. You don't have to follow a theme, but it can help to unify the garden visually and make a space feel more composed and restful. It can also be fun to create your own reality within the confines of the garden and let your imagination go. Do you want to feel as though you are stepping into your favourite holiday destination every time you go outside? A themed approach can make that happen. Specifically targeted projects are included in the design section and there is a note of where to find related projects throughout the book.

In view of the fact that many of us really are weekend gardeners with many other tasks and activities to cram into those two days, many of the garden design ideas are slanted towards easy maintenance. You can go a long way to add a certain flavour to the garden using props and appropriate paint colours, even before you think about plantings. And nowadays there are a number of products and techniques to cut down on basic maintenance such as weeding and watering without having to compromise on beauty and interest. Low maintenance need not mean dull and boring! Look through the different sections of the book to find out just what simple yet effective changes you can make to the whole of your garden, all in around a weekend or even less.

above: *Pots and containers bring easy versatility to any garden. There are numerous different types available and you can house many different plants in them, changing displays almost at will and moving containers around the garden to suit your mood.*

below: *Decking makes a good alternative surface in the garden.*

Creating a Garden

The patch of land adjacent to the house has the potential to become your own little bit of heaven, a sanctuary from the hurly burly of everyday life. Through television and magazine articles we are bombarded by images of perfect 'designer' gardens and the prospect of creating our own private green space can be a little daunting. But gardening is a deeply personal experience and all that really matters is that you make a garden to suit your needs and preferences.

Whether you are developing an existing site or creating something from scratch, you first need to consider practical matters such as budget, time available for construction and maintenance and how you plan to use the garden. Once that is sorted out you are free to let your imagination go and create your green idyll!

Selecting a theme for your garden

When space is limited, a garden needs a linking theme. Instead of planting and furnishing it with a random mixture of ideas, it pays to have a particular style in mind. That way, everything you do has a focus: the plants you buy, the pots, seating and paving all give out the same message. The result not only looks unified, but can also save you a great deal of money in plants and accessories that quickly lose their appeal when they do not look as good as you hoped once installed. A garden does not have to be fashionable to be stylish. What is fashionable may not look right for your home or neighbourhood, or suit the way you want to use your surroundings. An ultramodern, minimalist garden, for instance, would never look right around an old-fashioned cottage. But with thoughtful planning and good design you can often adapt unlikely styles to suit a range of different surroundings. For example, you could have a wild garden in the middle of town or a Japanese garden

below: *Traditional border perennials like lupins, delphiniums, foxgloves and* Dicentra spectabilis *provide a lovely cottagey display in early summer at about the time when roses begin to bloom in earnest. But some thought needs to be given to continuing the colour and interest for the rest of the season, when these showy, herbaceous plants have finished flowering.*

Do:

• Sketch a plan of the site and mark in any features that you wish to keep
• Go through gardening magazines and cut out pictures of plants and gardens that appeal
• Begin to draw together the key plants and decorative elements that strengthen your chosen theme
• Mark out the ground plan to help you visualize the design

Don't:

• Try to cram in too many different features. Simple designs work best
• Be too quick to discard existing trees and shrubs. They give the garden a feeling of maturity
• Ignore your surroundings. Choose a design that blends comfortably with the local architecture and landscape

left: This contemporary planting of drumstick alliums, herbs including chives, lavender, sage, artemisia and ornamental kale has a distinctly Mediterranean feel. The theme has been strengthened by placing a large terracotta jar in the midst of the flowers and foliage. Decorative elements such as this which have a simple outline, as well as large sculptural plants, can be used to provide a strong focal point and a visual 'anchor' in the garden.

below left: A pair of topiary swans in clipped box. Geometric topiary designs are strongly associated with formal gardens but simple animal shapes are also traditional elements of cottage gardens. Topiary has the reputation of being slow and difficult to train and expensive to buy, but there are ways to produce quite speedy results yourself.

outside an American or European city basement. And if you are worried that you might get bored with one distinctive style of garden, you can always divide up the space into smaller 'cameo' areas, each with its own identity. Alternatively, you could change part of the design or planting scheme every few years to give the garden a regular face-lift. Or even change the style completely, leaving only hard surfaces and other permanent features as the common factor. It is only practical to consider making such sweeping changes to a small garden, where plenty of style can be achieved with relatively little effort and cost.

Creating a cottage garden

A cottage garden is deliberately intended to look very natural, almost as if the flowers had appeared randomly all by themselves, without having been planted. This effect is partly achieved by growing plants that look 'in keeping', and partly by the way they are grown. Typical cottage garden plants include hardy annuals (violas, calendula and cornflowers), wild-looking perennials, such as hardy cranesbills, and cultivated forms of wildflowers, such as coloured primroses and violets. Equally authentic are culinary, decorative and medicinal herbs, shrub roses, flowering fruit trees, old-fashioned shrubs, such as myrtle and flowering quince, spring and summer bulbs, such as daffodils and lilies, and chrysanthemums and dahlias – originally grown for sale as cut flowers at the garden gate.

Natural Materials

Anything made of natural materials adds to the rustic character of a cottage garden. A wooden trug is ideal for gathering flowers or vegetables, or just for carrying light garden equipment, such as gloves, a trowel, secateurs and string. Look out, too, for willow or hazel plant supports of various types. Use rustic poles to make fencing, garden furniture or pillars and pergolas.

Related Projects

Hardy fuchsias *Most real old cottage garden plants were hardy, since cottagers were farm workers on low incomes and with no facilities such as greenhouses in which to keep tender plants through the winter.*

Tender perennials *Nowadays, a much larger range of tender plants have joined the ranks of cottage-style plants. Those with daisy flowers, such as argyranthemums and this Dendranthema 'White Gloss', look particularly at home.*

Pinks *Old varieties are valued as collector's plants. Their perfume is stronger than modern varieties, although the flowering period is shorter.*

Antirrhinum 'Liberty Cherry'

right: *The modern cottage garden is characterised by the softness and relaxed nature of its planting. It might include billowing grasses and other relative newcomers chosen for their similarity to wild flowers. But whatever you plant, don't forget to make full use of contrasting form and texture.*

Lavender   *Aromatic plants are a vital ingredient in the cottage garden mix, and lavender is an old favourite. It was once cultivated for the flowers which were dried and made into lavender bags, then kept in drawers of clothes to perfume them. It is one of many classic cottage garden plants that attracts butterflies and bees in huge numbers.*

Annuals   *Hardy annuals such as pansies were old cottage favourites, as they did not need any heat to raise, and many self seeded naturally, so did not make any work. However some half-hardy annuals also have the look.*

Watering can   *Props such as this old watering can add just the right finishing touch.*

Pansy

In old, original cottage gardens, plants were put in wherever there was a gap, with no thought for design or correct spacing. Spreading and self-seeding plants were allowed to ramble around at will, smothering out weeds and any plant unable to stand its ground, all of which contributed to the romantically disordered muddle. Today, many enthusiasts find a cottage garden is the ideal way to house a collection of choice 'treasures', which may be rare, old, named varieties of traditional plants, new perennials or even rock plants and miniature shrubs. These must be kept separate from the more invasive colonisers that would soon smother them. In the general mixed borders, plant randomly shaped swathes of smaller plants using odd numbers for groupings, for example three, five, seven and so on to give the display greater cohesion.

No fuss cottage flowers

Skill level:

Beginner gardener

Best time to do:

When the soil is dry

enough to rake over

Season:

Spring to midsummer

Special tools required:

A garden rake

A watering can or

hosepipe fitted with

a fine rose

WHAT YOU WILL NEED

• A range of hardy annual flower seeds (bought as separate packets)
• Some sand to mix with the seed and make it easy to handle
• A garden rake to prepare the ground
• A watering can with a fine rose
• A bamboo cane to make the drills

Hardy annuals are so quick and easy to grow from seed, they are ideal for filling in temporary gaps. Mix a variety of different kinds together and sow as one to produce a wildflower meadow effect. First remove any weeds, rake over the ground to form a fine tilth and then broadcast the seed/sand mixture. Water before sowing if the soil is dry. Or, for swathes of individual flowers, prepare the ground in the same way, mark out randomly shaped patches using a bamboo cane and sow a separate variety within each area. Make shallow grooves or seed drills with the cane and sow in rows so that you can spot the weed seedlings more easily.

SOWING MIXED ANNUAL SEEDS

Colourful, natural-look, random floral carpet effects are fashionable and easy to create, simply by mixing together a suitable 'palette' of seeds and broadcasting them over carefully prepared ground. Choose a good mixture of varieties with contrasting shapes and colours, but roughly similar heights. Use approximately equal quantities of each.

1 For an explosion of summer colour, mix together the seeds of a collection of annuals for sowing in one place.

Add the seeds to sand to bulk them up so that you can spread them more finely.

Californian poppy (Eschscholzia)

Red flax (Linum grandiflorum)

Shirley poppy (Papaver rhoeas)

Marigold (Calendula)   *Larkspur (Delphinium ajacis)*

Cornflower (Centaurea cy

2 The sand marks where you have scattered the seed. To prolong the display, make two sowings four weeks apart.

Right: *Calendula, cornflower and nigella are all non-invasive, self-seeding hardy annuals which are ideal for a cottage garden effect.*

GROWING BIENNIALS FROM SEED

To grow biennials from packets of seed, you must sow the seeds outdoors around early midsummer to have plants big enough to flower the following year. Biennials are normally sown in a row in a vacant patch in the vegetable garden, thinned out and transplanted to their flowering positions in early autumn. Alternatively, sow seed in trays outdoors and pot up singly.

1 Sprinkle seeds thinly into shallow drills made in rich, very fertile soil. On soil that dries out or forms a surface crust, cover the seed with vermiculite.

2 Rake very gently so that the seed is barely covered with soil. Water well, and do not allow soil to dry out; this could delay or prevent germination.

VARIATIONS ON THE THEME You could include elements that are reminiscent of gardens that once surrounded old manor houses on country estates. There is still an air of rustic simplicity but elements like closely mown lawns, clipped hedges and straight paths give greater definition.

Herbaceous borders *Perennials are usually seen against the backdrop of a yew hedge or an old, red brick wall. Since the original plants were mainly tall, a true country border would have needed a lot of staking and tying up. Nowadays there are compact versions of most traditional plants as well as relative newcomers like penstemons that need little attention.*

Perennial plants *A herbaceous border was a traditional feature of a country garden; classic plants, such as acanthus, lilies, alstroemeria, lupins (here 'Lulu Mixed') and delphiniums, were an essential part of the recipe.*

Country Character

Traditional features that evoke the atmosphere of a country garden include yew hedges; topiary; staddle stones; stone statues and urns as focal points (often formed by making a niche in an evergreen hedge); formal gardens within gardens; large lush lawns, including croquet lawns. All can be recreated on a small scale.

Traditional tools *A regular feature of genuine country gardens was the sight of gardeners at work in the grounds. You can recreate this feeling of activity by leaving old gardening tools about.*

Acanthus spinosus

Alstroemeria 'Orange Gem'

Lilium 'Talent'

Busy lifestyle garden

Time Saving

Keep track of the latest product innovations, as many are aimed specifically at people who want to garden well, but quickly. Slow-release fertilisers and feed sticks for containers, water-retaining gel crystals for hanging baskets and potting mixtures that last for a whole season.

Related Projects

- **Introducing pattern and texture pp 72–73**
- **Alternatives to grass pp 96–97**
- **Making a conifer and heather bed pp 100–101**
- **Garden decks and wooden surfaces pp 114–119**
- **Creating privacy with fence and trellis panels pp 140–141**
- **Raised pools and wall fountains pp 196–197**
- **Creating garden focal points pp 222–223**
- **Effects with glass beads and chippings pp 226–227**
- **Transformations with paints and stains pp 238–239**
- **Building garden seating pp 240–241**

Some styles of garden need plenty of regular attention to keep them looking good, but if quick and easy maintenance is your goal then make use of low-labour features and gardening aids. Low-maintenance gardens have the reputation of being rather dull and boring but there are plenty of ways of introducing colour and interest without having to rely on flowers. Decorative paving or decking plus mainly evergreen shrubs and ground cover plants can form an attractive framework for your urban sanctuary. Architectural features, such as topiary, sculpture and ornate but unplanted containers, add interest without making work. For extra variety, blend a mixture of surfaces underfoot, such as stone slabs, cobbles and old brick, to create contrasts with surrounding plants. You can cut down chores such as weeding by covering border soil with a deep mulch of bark chippings, compost or gravel to prevent annual weeds. But if starting from scratch, then the best plan is to lay perforated plastic sheeting or woven anti-weed fabric over the ground and plant through it, for permanent weed prevention.

Gaultheria mucronata

Rhododendron 'Salmon's Leap'

Calluna vulgaris 'Marleen'

above: *An alpine garden or scree bed provides an attractive and versatile use of low-maintenance gravel and boulders while at the same time offering scope for imaginative plantings. Alpine plants are hardy and easy to manage, adding to the appeal for those with busy lifestyles.*

Gravel and paving *Although more expensive to lay than grass, gravel and paving need considerably less upkeep than lawns and can create pleasing patterns and textures. An occasional rake-over or wash down in spring and some weedkiller is all that is needed.*

Leucothoe walteri 'Rainbow'

Containers or flower beds are most easily watered by installing a drip irrigation system. The most routine jobs in a low-labour garden are topping up mulches, cleaning paving and raking gravel. However, it usually takes quite a bit of time and effort to convert an existing garden to a low-maintenance format. Some people like to do the work in small stages over several years.

Choisya ternata 'Sundance'

Container plants *You can save time planting and replanting containers with new seasonal displays several times a year. Instead, plant slow-growing perennials or compact shrubs that can be left to thrive in the same container for several years.*

above: *Decking is an increasingly popular form of low-maintenance surface that can be used in any number of different garden contexts. It is practical, hard-wearing and relatively easy to keep in good condition.*

Change your approach: cut down work

Irrigation systems *Automatic irrigation, combined with a timer, can save hours of watering in summer. Fit containers with drip irrigation and lay perforated hoses through borders of newly establishing shrubs and flowers or through the vegetable plot. Do not bother watering the lawn – just raise the blades' cutting height in dry spells.*

In traditionally designed gardens, mowing, weeding and the watering of container-grown plants in summer are likely to be the major tasks. If you live in an area with lots of deciduous trees, the autumn fall can also create a temporary increase in the workload. One way to cut down on maintenance is to develop a more relaxed attitude and cheat a little! An untidy garden with weedy borders can be transformed by simply mowing and edging the lawn – it's a little like vacuuming the carpets indoors! A weekly mow keeps lawn weeds in check. When it comes to autumn leaves, enjoy the show for a while and only clear the lawns when the last batch has fallen. Forget tidying the borders before the winter – dead stems and leaves act as thermal insulation and it is easier to do the clear-up in spring. If you don't want to use bark mulch, weeding can be reduced to a minimum by thoroughly weeding in early spring, if necessary using a systemic weedkiller. Disturb the ground as little as possible during weeding or planting because every time you turn over the soil another batch of seeds is exposed to light, causing it to germinate. Close planting and the use of ground-cover varieties keeps soil shaded.

Hydrangea macrophylla

Santolina chamaecyparissus

Pachysandra terminalis

Weed prevention *You can avoid weeding entirely. When making a new bed, prepare the soil specially well, then cover it with a layer of perforated black plastic or special woven plastic mulching sheet. Plant shrubs and perennials through this, cutting crosses where they are to go, then tucking the flaps back closely around the stems. Cover the sheeting with a decorative mulch of bark chippings or gravel to hide it afterwards.*

Gaultheria procumbens

Leaky hose keeps border watered

above: *Natural stone slabs come in many different colours and hues, making them an attractive if expensive option for a low-maintenance garden floor. Spread gravel between the slabs and the decorative effect is heightened. This also enables planting between the slabs, to add a further dimension to the surface.*

VARIATIONS ON THE THEME In a small city garden the emphasis is switched from plants to decorating the garden's 'floors and walls'. Use decorative paving slabs and gravel for attractive, low-maintenance effects. Make the most of colour, using paints and stains to enliven woodwork and consider a mosaic feature for the ground. Introduce a piece of sculpture or a self-contained water feature as a focal point and make a permanent place to sit, to encourage you out into the garden in fine weather. Introduce greenery by planting up just a few large containers with evergreen shrubs, easy-care perennials and ground-cover plants. Meanwhile, use climbers such as honeysuckle, jasmine, ivy and clematis to cover trellis and perhaps to soften a pergola built for privacy. Plant climbers in the space provided by lifting a paving slab.

An oriental garden

Open Space

Oriental gardens are minimalist, so you need fewer ingredients than for a normal western-style garden. It is important that everything in the garden is perfectly placed and empty space is just as much a part of the design as the objects that frame it.

Related Projects

- **Making a gravel path pp 66–67**
- **Placing stepping stones in a lawn pp 92–93**
- **Soleirolia amongst pebbles pg 98**
- **Pebble, tile and brick surfaces pp 108–109**
- **Laying pebbles and cobbles including a 'dry' stream pp 110–111**
- **Erecting a pergola pp 146–147**
- **Self-contained and child-safe features pp 190–191**
- **Water features using hidden reservoirs pp 204–205**
- **Stone and ceramic spheres pp 246–247**
- **Innovative garden lighting pp 248–249**

An oriental-style garden contains characteristic ingredients: raked gravel, smooth stones and oriental-style ornaments, such as a bamboo deer scarer, a stone bridge over a dry 'river' of pebbles or a stone lantern. Added to these are a few typically architectural plants, such as bamboos, grasses, Japanese apricot, craggy conifers, Japanese maples and irises. You might also add shelves of small potted bonsai-style conifers, half hidden behind a bamboo screen. Oriental themes are ideal for low-labour small gardens because, lacking grass and traditional flower beds, they require very little maintenance. True oriental gardens are full of symbolism, and each individual rock is placed with great care and much thought, but the idea can be adapted to create various minimalistic gardens, including those known as 'dry gardens'. Zen gardens contain more rocks and gravel than plants, although on the whole most Westerners would probably prefer to add a few more plants.

below: *This Zen garden creates an atmosphere of peace and calm through its simplicity. In the foreground is a traditional stone water basin or tsukubai.*

Deer scarer *This is a traditional water feature that has long since lost its original use. Each time the swinging bamboo tube fills with water dripping from the narrow pipe, it tumbles, striking the rock and making a dull hollow thump.*

Plants with distinctive shapes *These are a feature of an oriental-style garden. Dwarf trees, especially those that can be trained and shaped and have an interesting outline.*

Craggy pines *The naturally craggy character of this blue pine,* Pinus leucodermis *'Blue Giant', is ideal for an oriental garden. It is a blue form of the Bosnian pine, an excellent species for a dry or chalky garden. Its drought-tolerant nature makes it suitable for growing in a container.*

Japanese umbrella pine *This* Sciadopitys verticillata *is a very slow-growing conifer that makes a striking shape and contrasts well with the other ingredients of an oriental garden. (It does not tolerate lime, so do not risk it on chalky gardens). Many typically oriental plants are evergreen.*

Bamboo *This is typically oriental-looking, but many kinds grow too big for a small garden. However this* Pleioblastus auricomus *stays compact enough to use in containers or in the ground where it spreads mildly. A small columnar bamboo reaching only 1.8m(6ft) in height is* Fargesia murieliae *'Simba'.*

Raked sand *Fine gravel or gritty granite sand is raked into patterns that may be interpreted as ripples on the water surface or waves in a stormy sea. Since the patterns are disturbed by birds or anyone walking over the garden, the sand needs raking regularly to keep the patterns intact.*

Planting oriental-style pots

Skill level:

Beginner gardener

Best time to do:

Any time of year, but

avoiding frost

Special tools required:

None

Time required:

Less than an hour, once

you have gathered all

the 'ingredients'

together

Compact evergreen shrubs, small magnolias, Japanese maples, slow-growing conifers such as dwarf pines, bamboos and grasses can all be grown in containers. And if you team these plants up with pots chosen for their oriental appeal it is easy to make a feature. Glazed pots are frost-proof and some come with matching feet (for winter drainage) or saucers (for use during summer). Plain coloured glazed pots, for example deep blue or jade green, work well with most schemes, but you can also buy lacquer red pots for a theatrical touch. Designs range from simple leaf-motifs to stylised dragons. Bamboos instantly add an Eastern flavour. Choose carefully as some are very vigorous. Try forms of the columnar *Fargesia* and *Phyllostachys* and creeping *Pleioblastus* varieties.

1 Put a crock over the drainage hole in the base of the pot to stop the potting mix running out when you water the container.

2 Add 2.5cm(1in) of coarse grit or fine gravel for drainage and to prevent soil from trickling out through the drainage hole.

3 Knock the plant out of its pot. If it is difficult to dislodge, tap the side of the pot firmly onto a hard surface to loosen it.

WHAT YOU WILL NEED

• A large glazed pot, either plain or decorated with a simple oriental motif
• A small-growing bamboo
• A flat stone, piece of broken clay pot, or chunks of broken up polystyrene plant trays
• Coarse grit or fine gravel
• Potting compost
• Matching 'feet' to raise the pot off the ground

4 Sit the plant in the middle of its pot. The top of the rootball should come to about 2.5cm(1in) below the rim of the pot. If not, lift it out and either add or remove soil to bring it to the correct level.

5 Fill the gap between the rootball and the sides of the container with more of the same potting mixture and firm it in very lightly to make sure that the pot is completely filled. Move the pot to its final position and water well.

CREATING AN ORIENTAL DISPLAY

If aiming at an oriental effect, use a 'nest' of similar containers of different sizes – each planted with a single type of plant only – and position them so that they form a group, consisting of a flowering plant, a foliage plant and a shrub or small tree. Add a bamboo wind chime for sound effects resembling a mountain stream, and for added authenticity, stand the pots on raked gravel or plain paving with a leafy foliage or architectural background. Add some large rounded cobbles and smaller pebbles to 'anchor' the collection.

Useful Conifers

Many other striking conifers complement the oriental style; look for low, dome-shaped pines such as Pinus mugo 'Gnom'; pines with very long, blue needles, such as Pinus griffithii; ground-hugging junipers and Cryptomeria japonica cultivars for their bronze-red winter colouring. Also choose conifers that look like natural bonsais and duplicate the shape of old gnarled or weathered trees.

Miscanthus sinensis 'Zebrinus'

1 Place crocks over the holes in the bottom of each pot, then partly fill them all with a good-quality, soil-based potting mixture.

2 Knock the plants out of their pots, teasing out some of the largest roots if necessary. Lift each plant into a suitably sized pot.

Cryptomeria japonica 'Spiralis'

Picea glauca 'Alberta Globe'

3 Put the plants in position. Spread 2.5cm(1in) of gravel over the area around them, ideally over compacted soil, concrete or some other hard surface. Add a group of large pebbles or cobble-stones. Press them down slightly so that they stay put without appearing to sink. This kind of display would provide the perfect focus for a tiny basement garden or an enclosed courtyard.

above: *The oriental look is relatively easy to reproduce with a suitable small pine tree, some striking silver-grey boulders and plenty of gravel. Stones featuring Japanese characters can also be acquired to enhance the effect.*

Making a pebble feature

Skill level:

Some gardening and

DIY experience an

advantage

Best time to do:

Mid-spring to early

autumn

Special tools required:

Possibly a hammer and

chisel

Time required:

Half a day

Here, large rounded boulders and smaller cobbles are arranged together and drought-tolerant plants added to complement them. This scheme could add interest to a large area of gravel such as a drive, but make sure you choose a spot where it does not interfere with pedestrians or car parking. Or try it within a patio, in a space where several paving slabs have been lifted out. For the feature to look more oriental, always lift an odd number of slabs and make the area irregular in outline. Insert the plants through the hard foundation, mixing some garden compost into the planting hole to help with establishment. Alternatively, leave a patch of bare soil to develop as a feature when laying the patio. If you do this, cover the soil with an anti-weed mulch fabric, plant through this and carefully disguise the mulch with gravel. A feature like this has a definite 'front' and should face the direction from which it is most often seen. Otherwise, design the feature so that the largest stones and tallest 'key' plants are positioned towards the centre, with smaller groups and creeping plants radiating outwards.

WHAT YOU WILL NEED

• A selection of dwarf and prostrate growing conifers
• Drought-tolerant herbs and ground-cover plants, especially alpines. Include mainly evergreens
• Boulders, cobbles, pebbles
• Well-rotted garden compost or good quality potting mix
• Possibly a hammer and chisel
• Washed sand
• Gravel mulch

1 Arrange a group of large rounded boulders on a base of rubble topped with washed building sand. Choose several similarly coloured stones and one much larger in a different colour as a contrast. Lay a randomly shaped patch of similar looking cobbles onto the sand near the main group. Try adding a plant such as *Juniperus squamata* 'Blue Star' between the biggest stones to 'anchor' things.

2 Position remaining plants, making sure that you have a good mix of contrasting textures, habit and leaf colours. Even if you choose some flowering alpines, foliage is crucial. Try to arrange in a natural way so that plants 'nestle' amongst the stones. Begin to excavate the holes to reach the soil below. You may need a hammer and chisel to break up the rubble. Add some handfuls of compost.

3 Water, then remove pots and begin to plant, lifting up trails of foliage so that they lie on top of the sand. Firm in with your hands. Once planted, apply a generous dressing of pea gravel rather than stone chippings which can look rather artificial. Tuck the gravel beneath the foliage of carpeting alpines and herbs taking it right around the necks. This helps to conserve moisture and cut down weeds.

Suitable Trees

Where space permits, a small tree with an oriental feel would provide a lovely focal point. As well as having a strikingly architectural profile or ornamental bark, it needs to be capable of withstanding full sun and sharp drainage. An ideal choice would be one of the cut-leaved sumachs such as Rhus typhina *'Dissecta', with excellent autumn colour. You could also use the strawberry tree,* Arbutus unedo *or the hybrid* A. × andrachnoides *with cinnamon-red peeling bark.*

Stones *Garden centres now supply bags of graded pebbles, cobbles and smooth boulders. You can also buy stone chippings and gravel in various grades and colours. For a Zen dry garden or karesansui, you might only find the right shapes and sizes at a specialist stone merchant.*

Conifers *The striking, asymmetrical form of certain conifers perfectly complements this style of gardening. Combine those having a naturally arching, ground-hugging or more upright growth habit. One particularly unusual specimen conifer can be used as a focal point and to strengthen the oriental feel. Try weeping conifers such as* Cedrus atlantica *'Glauca Pendula'.*

Perennials *Balance the conifer grouping with lower-growing evergreen, perennials such as* Verbascum *'Jackie' and sea holly (*Eryngium variifolium*). Contrast leaf shapes and textures by adding in tussock-forming grasses like* Festuca. *And for creeping ground cover, try alpines including thymes and the daisy-flowered* Rhodanthemum hosmariense.

Juniperus squamata
'Blue Alps'

Festuca glauca
'Golden Toupee'

Juniperus communis
'Depressa Aurea'

Eryngium
variifolium

Rhodanthemum hosmariense

Dianthus
'Spring Star'

Two easy bonsai projects

WHAT YOU WILL NEED

- Shallow bonsai containers
- Juniper cutting, e.g. a starter plant from garden centre
- A selection of small beech cuttings, e.g. hedging
- Long-nosed scissors
- Fairly thick galvanised wire
- Fine, soil-based potting mix
- Clay and fine-milled peat
- Rolled card to make a soil scoop
- Moss and fine grit for decoration

Both of the techniques shown here produce almost instant results and are a great way to learn about bonsai without spending a lot of money on tools, equipment and plants. Junipers are ideal candidates but you can experiment with pruning and wiring all kinds of small-leaved shrubs. Make a special place in your Oriental garden for the plants, displaying them on a simple wooden shelf or tiered bench. Bear in mind that you must be able to water regularly during the summer months because there is such a small soil volume that plants dry out very quickly.

A JUNIPER BONSAI

This sequence features a two-year-old cutting of Juniperus squamata 'Meyeri'. Its compact foliage allows it to be formed into an almost instant bonsai subject. Deciduous species need two or three years.

1 Clear all the foliage and small shoots from the trunk, leaving the larger branches. Try to avoid leaving opposite branches.

2 Do not let the size of the original plant dictate the size of the bonsai. Cut off one of the twin leaders and shorten the other.

3 With the trunk and wire held together, begin to coil. Hold close to where you are coiling and move your hand as you progress.

4 Grasp as much of the trunk as possible to spread the pressure and bend it into the desired shapes and curves.

5 Bend the branches down, ensuring there are a few at the back. Bend close to the trunk. Clear any growth facing down. After a couple of hours, the juniper looks like a little tree. In time, the foliage pads will fill out. Unwind and reapply wire as the trunk thickens.

1 These beech cuttings are not particularly inspiring at first sight, but their different thicknesses and lines are just right for creating a group. Hedging is ideal.

2 Prepare each cutting in turn. Cut away the long roots with sharp scissors, leaving as many fine feeder roots as possible. These will nourish the young tree.

3 Work a sticky mixture of equal parts of clay and fine peat between the roots and mould it into a ball. Do this for each of the cuttings featured in the group.

4 The clay balls keep the trees in position while they are being arranged in the pot. Start with the tallest tree, just off-centre, and place the two next tallest ones either side.

5 When the arrangement is complete, add soil between the clay balls covering the root masses. Dry soil is easier to apply as it does not stick to the wet clay. To make the job easier, make a scoop from rolled card.

6 Complete by 'landscaping' the soil surface with different kinds of moss and grit. Water the pot and moss first, and avoid pressing the moss down too hard.

7 The new beech group planting is already pleasing to the eye. Note how the trees at the edges of the group have been pruned so that each apex sweeps outwards. Continue to prune as the trees grow maintaining a natural profile. After two years prune the roots and refill with fresh compost.

Varying the spaces between the trees produces a more natural effect.

Making a wild garden

Wildflowers

Include groups of wildflowers among shrubs. Choose those that suit the soil and situation. Low-growing wildflowers, such as cowslips or primroses, violets and trefoils, look good grown in grass; mow short paths for access through longer grass that is only cut twice a year, in early spring and autumn.

Related Projects

- **No fuss cottage flowers pg 16**
- **Making a gravel path pp 66–67**
- **Variations: Seaside pebbles pg 71**
- **Placing stepping stones in a lawn pp 92–93**
- **Fencing for the country-style garden pp 144–145**
- **Encouraging wildlife with water pp 194–195**
- **A miniature water lily pond pp 200–201**
- **Installing a pond pp 206–207**
- **Making a bog garden pp 216–217**
- **Making a wildlife water feature pp 218–219**

A wild garden is not simply a normal one that has been left to run wild. It is a slice of the countryside recreated specially, using native trees shrubs and flowers planted in a very naturalistic style. Since there are no rules for wild gardening, you can also decorate the garden with cultivated flowers, though for authenticity it looks best to use those that are close cousins of wild plants. 'Accessories' such as fallen logs and tree stumps, rocks, pebbles, bark chippings and a shallow pool can all be used to colour the scene, depending on the local landscape. For instance, on a heavily wooded site, a woodland-style garden will look most at home. You could create a small clearing and have a tree surgeon thin a dense canopy of branches to allow more light in so that a greater range of plants will grow. On a hot dry sunny site, a wild style that uses rocks and drought-tolerant plants will look most natural. In a damp garden, a pond flanked by moisture-loving plants with hazels and willows looks the part. And in a more normal garden, you could create a meadow-style garden with mixed hedgerows,

Birdfeeders *Place a bird table within easy reach of trees and shrubs to which birds can quickly escape if a predator threatens. Feed peanuts in hanging net containers; use squirrel-proof containers if these or other rodents are a problem. Feed a mixture of bird seeds of various sizes so that there is something for a wide variety of different birds. You can also buy ready-made bird cake containing fat and seeds.*

Nestboxes *To attract birds to nest in the garden, put up nestboxes; different sized openings are available to suit various birds. Place the boxes above head height, in a sheltered place safe from cats and other predators; under the eaves of a shed or on a tree trunk facing away from the prevailing wind. Some birds will also nest in containers lodged firmly on their sides amongst tight-knit branches in a hedge.*

Feeding the Birds

Feed birds from autumn through winter until late spring when their natural sources of food are scarce. The birds in your garden will come to rely on you, so try to ensure for their sakes that there is always a regular supply of food. Clean, non-frozen drinking and bathing water is also essential.

left: *A wildflower meadow – which can be as tiny as you like, to suit the size of your garden – has great ecological value and looks good, too.*

Small trees and shrubs with fruit or berries provide a good source of food for birds in autumn and winter, for example red-berried holly, cotoneaster, sorbus and the Viburnum opulus *shown here.*

Rhus typhina 'Dissecta'

Ilex aquifolium 'Alaska'

Rubus 'Betty Ashburner'

a shallow pond or even a running stream with pebbled banks and drifts of shrubs and flowers. It is also possible to create a conventional garden with informal beds and borders planted with native species and wilder-looking cultivated flowers. A natural garden attracts wildlife, as it supplies plenty of food, plus drinking and bathing facilities and is relatively easy to look after. When selecting plants, include those that are favourites with insects including bees, moths and butterflies. Happily these very often include scented, nectar-rich varieties like the different coloured forms of *Buddleja davidii*. All kinds of herbs are popular, and beneficial insects such as hoverflies are drawn to dish-shaped or daisy-style flowers. Dragonflies, bats and birds will be attracted by the increased insect activity.

Achieving a natural effect

Skill level:

Beginner gardener

Best time to do:

As soon as bulbs are

available

Special tools required:

Sharp border spade;

hand cultivator; trowel;

garden rake

Time required:

Depends on the area of

lawn to be planted

WHAT YOU WILL NEED

• Bulbs suitable for naturalising. Selected for sun or shade
• Sharp border spade
• Hand cultivator or border fork
• Trowel or bulb planter
• Garden rake
• Optional – grit to lighten heavy soil or well-rotted compost to improve poor, dry soil

There are bulbs to suit any and every situation in the garden, but for a natural effect, you need to choose the different kinds carefully. Large-flowered daffodils, fancy tulips and hybrid gladioli will look out of place in a natural scheme and unlike dwarf and small-flowered kinds do not die back very gracefully after flowering. When planting in drifts, avoid multi-coloured mixtures. There are many bulbs that thrive in shady locations, including the dainty dwarf daffodils, wood anemones, snowdrops, snowflakes (*Leucojum aestivum*), *Cyclamen coum* and *C. hederifolium*, scillas and bluebells. Plant in random groupings or large drifts in lawns, beneath trees, along the base of hedges and to give early colour through borders of deciduous shrubs and herbaceous perennials. In the first year the display may look quite thin, but most bulbs bulk up quite rapidly. Just keep adding a few more each year. To plant for a natural effect, just dig a fairly wide hole to the correct depth and plant a number of bulbs at the same time.

right: *Crocuses make little foliage and do not 'swamp' the grass. Delay mowing until six weeks after the bulb foliage has died down. Avoid lawn feeds with weedkillers where bulbs are naturalised. Use Dutch crocus as well as the early-flowering C. tommasinianus.*

below: *Daffodils are perfect for naturalising in grass. Mow the lawn in midwinter so that the flowers are not swamped by long grass. Then delay mowing again until six weeks after the flowers are over. For smaller, more natural looking flowers, go for cyclamineus daffodils. These are some of the first to bloom.*

NATURALISING BULBS IN GRASS

One of the prettiest ways to grow spring bulbs is naturalised in grass. The most suitable types are those that are happy to be left undisturbed, such as narcissi and crocus, but many small bulbs are suitable, although hyacinths and tulips are not. Plant narcissi and crocus bulbs in natural 'drifts' (well-defined areas where bulbs are planted closely together) in an ornamental lawn to add spring interest.

1 Mark an area with a sharp spade and slide the blade beneath the turf to sever the roots. Roll back the turf.

2 Loosen the soil as deeply as possible. Add well-rotted and sieved organic matter to poor soil and grit to heavy soil.

3 Scatter the bulbs (crocus, in this case) and plant them wherever they fall. Scoop out enough soil to plant each bulb at the right depth.

4 Roll the turf back and firm it down lightly – the whole turf must touch the soil below. Water the area if the weather is dry and keep it moist.

Buddleja davidii 'Pink Delight'

Rhamnus frangula 'Aspleniifolia'

Eupatorium purpureum maculatum

Sambucus nigra 'Madonna'

Vaccinium 'Red Pearl'

Aegopodium podagraria 'Variegatum'

Ajuga reptans 'Braunherz'

VARIATIONS ON THE THEME All of the plants illustrated are grown principally for their ornamental value but each also attracts a variety of wildlife. Bumble bees enjoy the blue flowers of the *Ajuga* and all kinds of insects, especially butterflies, will home in on the *Buddleja* and other nectar rich flowers like Joe Pye Weed (*Eupatorium*). The *Vaccinium*, *Rhamnus* and elderberry (*Sambucus*) pictured here all produce berries.

A woodland glade

Leafmould

This accumulates under trees in wild woodland, forming a deep, rich, naturally lime-free soil. At home, collect dead leaves and rot them down in a leafmould cage or for speedier results, in sealed, heavy-duty refuse sacks. Leafmould is particularly useful for enriching the soil prior to planting acid-loving woodlanders such as deciduous azaleas.

A garden that has a thriving population of trees can be developed – without any major clearing and replanting – as an attractive woodland-style garden. This is true regardless of whether the trees concerned are wild native species or ornamental garden varieties. In fact, this theme is a good way of restyling a small garden that has previously been rather overplanted with trees. There is no reason why the foundation of your woodland should not be, for example, flowering cherries. Natural woodland normally needs clearing of brambles, unwanted saplings of weed species such as sycamore, and similar scrub before you can start planting. Old woodland also has its own build-up of rich, fertile leafmould that needs little improvement. Elsewhere, prepare the soil well by mulching with large quantities of well-rotted organic matter, since the sort of plants that thrive in woodland like humus-rich soil and usually prefer lime-free conditions. Plant 'drifts' of choice woodland ground cover plants.

above: *A short flight of stone steps in a path that winds through woodland planting becomes a feature in its own right. After a while you will find that all kinds of wild woodlanders begin to colonise, softening hard landscaping features.*

Choice woodland plants *Moist, fertile, leafmould-rich soil and light shade provide superb growing conditions for a great many choicer woodland plants, such as* Corydalis flexuosa, *shown here. Violets, hardy cyclamen, hellebores, lily-of-the-valley and epimediums all enjoy the same conditions, and many can be quite difficult to grow elsewhere.*

Hardy ferns *Hardy ferns are known for their delicate lacy foliage and fondness for shady woodland conditions. Most, such as the lady fern* (Athyrium filix-femina), *thrive best in moist shade. However, the soft shield fern* (Polystichum setiferum 'Congestum'), *shown here, likes fertile, humus-rich, but well-drained soil that is not too wet in winter. A few, including* Dryopteris *species, thrive in dry shade; they are useful for growing under large trees, whose roots take up a lot of the moisture.*

Cornus controversa 'Variegata' *The wedding cake tree makes a tiered shape, with branches forming distinct layers outlined in cream-and-green foliage. This striking small tree or large shrub only thrives where it is sheltered by surrounding trees, and is seen at its best in light woodland.*

right: Acer palmatum atropurpureum *and* Vitis coignetiae *are perfect companions for an autumn display, with their striking end-of-summer colour. However, always ensure that they are planted in a suitable setting.*

Ground cover *For mass ground cover in a woodland garden, choose decorative, low-growing, but tough, spreading plants.* Rubus calycoides *'Betty Ashburner' and the variegated ground elder (*Aegopodium podagraria *'Variegatum'), are ideal.*

Rubus calycoides 'Betty Ashburner'

Grasslike plants *The variegated woodrush (*Luzula sylvatica *'Aureomarginata') makes attractive tussocks.*

Athyrium filix-femina (lady fern)

Blechnum spicant

Woodland garden surfaces *Grass does not grow happily in the shade of a woodland garden; instead, use a surface of bark chippings.*

Creating a Mediterranean garden

Scented Herbs

These play a great part in creating a Mediterranean-style ambience. Drought-proof evergreen thyme, rosemary and ornamental sages are both decorative and also useful in the kitchen. To make the most of aromatic herbs, plant creeping thymes in cracks in the paving on a patio where they will occasionally be walked on. Group terracotta pots planted individually with sages, rosemary, winter savory, common thyme, bay and stong-flavoured Greek oregano in full sun close to the house. In a shady corner, stand pots containing some of the many kinds of mint. You can also grow herbs in rough-sawn wooden window boxes or plant up baskets and wall pots to hang at nose level.

Related Projects

- **Laying random stone pp 82–83**
- **Planning a Mediterranean gravel garden pp 104–105**
- **Mosaics and pebble patterns pp 112–113**
- **The terracotta terrace pp 162–163**
- **Creating colourful backdrops pp 236–237**
- **Painting pots and planters pp 228–229**

A totally paved garden is ideal for a hot or dry climate where grass does not thrive, but also makes an attractive low-maintenance garden that maximises a small space. It could form a complete garden, or be one feature of several within a larger garden. The essence of this style of small garden is wall space and containers. Climbers are best grown up a pergola, trellis or netting; wall-trained shrubs can be tied up to horizontal wires secured to special wall nails. Either way, it is a good idea to use plant supports that hold stems well away from the wall to allow for good air circulation. Wall plants may be grown in narrow beds left at the foot of walls when laying paving, but thorough soil preparation is essential, since soil in this situation is naturally very dry and impoverished. Containers, including

Compact shrubs *Good, compact shrubs for a Mediterranean-style border in a small garden include potentilla, cistus and hebe. More unusual dwarf shrubs include* Lotus hirsutus *and* Convolvulus cneorum.

Anisodontea capensis 'Sapphire' (half-hardy perennial)

Hebe 'Sapphire' (shrub)

Suitable plants *Drought-tolerant, sunloving plants are the most practical kind to grow in containers in a warm sunny spot. Pelargoniums, anisodontea and portulaca all make a good show, and have the typical, brightly coloured flowers of Mediterranean gardens. Also try daisy-flowered marguerites.*

Lotus hirsutus (shrubby perennial)

Portulaca 'Sundial Mixed' (half-hardy annual)

Salvia officinalis 'Purpurea' (hardy perennial herb)

Gazania 'Daybreak' (half-hardy perennial)

Terracotta and natural wood *Terracotta pots and natural, untreated wooden boxes complete the Mediterranean style; all team up well with plain stone or concrete paving.*

left: *This sunny, paved corner has all the hallmarks of a Mediterranean garden. A jumble of plants are grouped together, grown in a wide assortment of terracotta pots. They include drought tolerant bedding – helichrysum and geranium – as well as succulents and flowering bulbs. The sword shaped leaves of a variegated agave make a striking centrepiece.*

hanging baskets, wall planters and tubs and troughs, are the popular way of adding seasonal colour and changing interest to a garden of this type. However, they need regular watering, feeding and deadheading to keep plants flowering well, and this can be a problem for people who are out all day. Containers can be fitted with an automatic watering system but take care not to overwater sun-loving herbs. Grow drought tolerant plants, such as *Acaena* (New Zealand bur), prostrate junipers, whipcord hebe, dwarf lavender, creeping thyme and *Rhodanthemum hosmariense* in cracks between paving or where paving slabs have been removed to make a small bed mulched with gravel.

A Riviera touch

Skill level:

Some experience of

clipping or training

plants useful, but not

essential

Best time to do:

Spring through to late

summer

Special tools required:

Secateurs

Time required:

Just an hour or two

WHAT YOU WILL NEED

• Bay tree (*Laurus nobilis*) with
a single, straight central stem
• Three or five bamboo canes
plus twine to secure wigwam
• Secateurs
• Piece of stiff wire for adjustable
circular loop
• Terracotta pot and free-draining
compost to pot into

Where the Mediterranean look is fairly relaxed – perhaps reminiscent of a garden in a little Greek island fishing village, the Riviera style is rather smarter and more upmarket. Instead of a motley collection of old olive oil cans painted up for use as plant pots, you are more likely to see large ornate terracotta containers, carved stone ornaments and balustrading. The planting is similar but far more flamboyant with lots of exotica. Use plants with bold sculptural leaves and large colourful blooms. Those on the borders of hardiness often have the right look, though tend to need more work to protect them in winter. Plant in pots so that they can be moved under cover in autumn or be prepared to wrap up tender shrubs, tree ferns and palms using plenty of horticultural fleece. Mulching tender bulbs, tubers and herbaceous plants with a thick layer of free-draining material insulates the roots. Use the same approach with tender climbers like *Eccremocarpus scaber* and *Campsis* varieties. Some annuals and tender perennial bedding plants work well in Riviera style plantings, including bronze-leaved *Ricinus communis*, *Fuchsia* 'Thalia' and *Cleome spinosa*. Incorporate a little formal pool with a sparkling fountain and include appropriate props like ornate ironwork wall lamps, reproduction stone urns and wooden steamer chairs.

left: *Oranges and lemons are so much a part of the Mediterranean landscape and if you have a glass house or conservatory where they can be overwintered, you could grow them in your garden. In summer it is best to stand citrus outside on a sunny patio, bringing them back under cover in autumn. Left unchecked they make untidy plants, so prune to form attractive short, round-headed standards on a single trunk. Grow named grafted plants preferably from specialist nurseries. Many are everbearing, which means that the fragrant flowers and fruits appear at the same time.*

Callistemon citrinus
'Splendens'

Acacia dealbata

Cordyline australis
'Atropurpurea'

Abutilon
'J. Morris'

Phygelius
capensis

Phormium tenax
'Pink Panther'

Solanum crispum
'Glasnevin'

Subtropical flavour   *There are plenty of exotic style shrubs and perennials that look the part and yet are reasonably hardy. Handsome foliage plants play a big part in the Riviera look – pick those with large leaves or bold architectural shapes. Bamboo, phormium and cordyline,* Fatsia japonica, *Chusan palm (*Trachycarpus fortunei*) and yuccas make fine additions. For summer highlights plant up big terracotta pots with luscious flowering plants – coloured arum lilies, cannas, abutilons and bottlebrushes (*Callistemon*). Smother warm sunny walls with flowering climbers. Finish the look with a few props such as colonial-style furniture.*

TRAINING A BAY TREE

Bay trees are traditionally trained into ornamental shapes, such as standard 'lollipops' or cones. They are often grown in terracotta pots by a doorway or on a patio or used to decorate a formal herb garden.

1 Slip a tripod of canes over the tree. Encircle it with an adjustable wire hoop to help you achieve an even conical shape. Using secateurs, neatly snip away any shoots that extend beyond the conical outline. Move the wire hoop as you work. Use the trimmed leaves for cooking!

2 Pinch out the tips of young shoots growing towards the edges of the desired shape. Bay leaves are quite large and would be spoiled if they were cut in half.

3 The end result is a smartly trimmed tree. Do not expect a totally smooth outline as you would get with a clipped small-leaved plant.

A small alpine garden

Variegated Leaves

Plants that flower early and then have good variegated foliage for the rest of the season are well worth their place in a rock garden; Arabis ferdinandi-coburgi 'Variegata' can be found in most good garden centres. It has short white spikes of flowers in spring.

Related Projects

- **Making a gravel path pp 66–67**
- **Variations: seaside pebbles pg 71**
- **Laying random stone pp 82–83**
- **Planting green carpets pp 98–99**
- **Planting bulbs under gravel pg 105**
- **Versatile and decorative gravel pp 102–103**
- **Livening up your patio pp 106–107**
- **Succulents in plain terracotta pg 163**
- **Installing fountains and waterfalls pp 214–215**
- **Effects with glass beads and chippings pp 226–227**

Keen plant enthusiasts, limited to a small garden, can often make better use of the space than the person with a large garden but only limited funds to develop it. One way of making the most of a tiny area is to grow naturally small plants, and to choose a style of garden that allows all the available space to be used for beds instead of being taken up by lawns. An alpine garden is a good example. Here, everything is on a small scale. The garden consists of wall-to-wall plant beds, filled with a huge variety of rock plants, dwarf bulbs and miniature shrubs, decorated with chunks of rock and topdressed with fine gravel. This makes a good background to the plants, as well as providing well-drained growing conditions. Narrow stone-flagged or gravel paths wind between rocky outcrops to provide access for enjoyment and essential jobs such as weeding and watering. A seating area outside the patio doors can continue the alpine theme, with stone slabs and sink gardens planted with more rock plants. Hardwood benches or stone seats and tables look the part and can be left out all year round. Enthusiasts may also like to have a cold frame or small unheated greenhouse.

SUMMER COLOUR

The vast majority of well-known alpines, such as saxifrages and dwarf bulbs, are spring flowering. To keep containers like sink gardens looking good for a longer season, it is vital to include some later colour as well. Good plants for summer flowers include small species of phlox, erodium, geranium, sedum and dianthus, plus rhodohypoxis. All alpines growing in containers need watering regularly during prolonged dry spells; even they can be killed by drought. And since plants will be growing in the same container for several years, apply weak liquid feeds several times during the summer months.

above: *Summer flowering phlox and dianthus spilling over the side of this sink garden coincide with the last of the saxifrages to create a display that always has something in flower but never looks garish.*

Summer-flowering species *The vast majority of rock plants flower in spring, so to keep the rockery looking colourful, choose plenty of plants with summer flowers and long flowering seasons. Good ones include* Campanula cochleariifolia *(shown here),* Helianthemum, Campanula carpatica *'Blue Clips',* Parahebe catarractae, *and* Gypsophila repens *'Rosea'.*

Drought-resistant sunlovers *Silver foliage plants, such as this* Artemisia schmidtiana *'Nana', and those with succulent leaves, such as* Sedum spathulifolium *'Cape Blanco' and* Sempervivum *'Commander Hay', are naturally drought-resistant, ideal for the most sun-baked situations where many other rock plants fail.*

Low spreading plants *Many rock plants are clump-forming, so include a few low spreading kinds that wander about the garden without becoming a nuisance. They provide a visual link between islands of plants that would otherwise look adrift in a sea of gravel.* Pratia pedunculata *(shown here) is ideal. It grows just 3cm(1.2in) high and has pale blue flowers.*

Rock pinks *These have silvery-blue foliage with mini carnation-like flowers.*

Helianthemum 'Rose of Leeswood'

Sedum spathulifolium 'Cape Blanco'

Parahebe catarractae

Arabis fernandi-coburgi 'Variegata'

Gypsophila repens 'Rosea'

Dwarf trees *Mini trees, such as this woolly willow (*Salix lanata*), look naturally stunted and add an authentic air to a rock garden. It grows to a maximum of 90cm(36in) high, and has fat yellowish-grey catkins in spring and felty-textured, grey, disc-shaped leaves. These are shed in winter.*

Campanula carpatica 'Blue Clips'

Rocks *To create the most natural rock feature without using rock taken from the wild, choose old local stone recycled from another rockery where possible. Alternatively, use reconstituted stone.*

Lewisias *These have colourful long-lasting flowers. The plants like a hot sunny spot with very well-drained gritty soil. As they are unusually susceptible to rotting off at the neck, plant them in a rock crevice, with the rosettes of foliage facing sideways instead of upright. these are* Lewisia *'Ashwood Mixed'.*

Grit *To mulch a rock feature, use fine gravel or grit to a depth of 2.5-5cm (1-2in). Tuck this under plants to improve surface drainage and prevent collar rot. Top up by sprinkling more grit between plants after tidying the rock garden in autumn.*

Planting a sink garden with alpines

Few people have room for conventional rockeries and there is also growing concern about the removal of rock from natural habitats for use in gardens. The most practical alternative, especially where space or funds are limited, is to grow alpines in containers. This way you avoid using any natural rock at all, as the hard surface of the container provides a suitable backdrop. The traditional container for alpines was an old-fashioned stone butler's sink, but you can adapt modern sinks by covering them with hypertufa. This is a mix of equal parts by volume of cement, gritty sand and moss peat with water to mix into a firm paste. Use wire wool to rough up the surface of the sink and then cover with tile adhesive to help the hypertufa to bond. Sink-type containers must have drainage holes in the bottom. Most alpines will thrive in a free-draining mixture with some organic matter to hold moisture. You may need to prepare this at home, as suitable mixes are normally only sold by specialist alpine plant nurseries. More moisture-loving plants, such as tiny alpine primulas, Dodecatheon, Ramonda, etc., are happy in a mixture of equal parts soil- and peat-based potting mix. Be sure to group plants that will happily share similar growing conditions. Most alpines will thrive in a situation where they get direct sun for at least half the day, although very drought-tolerant, sunloving kinds such as sedums and sempervivums need a very sunny spot. Few alpines are happy in shade; go for Ramonda, Haberlea and dwarf ferns. Water sink gardens in dry weather, and feed plants occasionally in spring and summer with weak tomato feed.

WHAT YOU WILL NEED

- Alpine trough
- Crocks for drainage
- Special lime-free gritty compost
- Narrow bladed trowel
- Selection of plants
- Small rock pieces for decoration
- Fine alpine gravel or granite chippings
- Bricks to raise trough

1 Cover the drainage holes with crocks. These prevent soil from running out but allow excess water to drain away freely.

2 Almost fill the sink with equal parts of lime-free gritty sand, soil-based mix and coir, coarse peat or sterilised leafmould.

3 Decide on the arrangement and start from the centre. Tip each plant out of its pot and use a small trowel to scoop out a hole.

4 Nestle plants into the corners so the sink has a well-filled but natural look. Make sure a few plants trail over to soften the sides.

5 Choose a few small pieces of attractive stone and tuck them in amongst the plants as you work. These add contours, trap condensation in hot weather and help to keep plant roots cool. Use plants with long flowering seasons and some, such as mossy saxifrages, that make good background foliage when not in bloom. Mix plants with contrasting shapes and textures.

6 Use a narrow-bladed trowel to make holes for plants and pieces of stone. Avoid damaging the rootballs of nearby plants. Don't forget that you can also plant tiny alpine bulbs and tubers such as some of the species crocus, daffodils and tulips.

7 When all the plants and rocks are in place, spread a generous layer of gravel or granite chippings over the whole surface as a stone mulch.

8 The sink garden looks good straight away, but will improve as plants blend together and spill over the sides. Water well and raise up on bricks for extra drainage – a vital consideration.

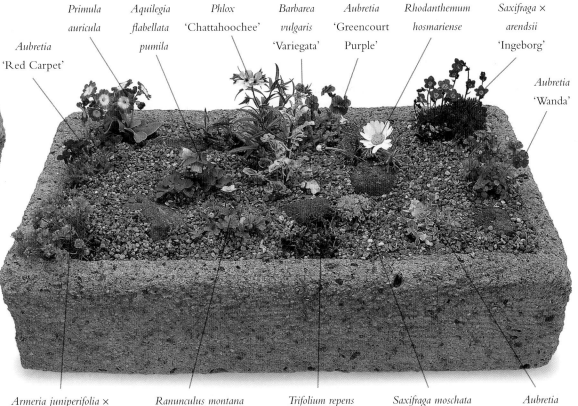

Primula auricula

Aquilegia flabellata pumila

Phlox 'Chattahoochee'

Barbarea vulgaris 'Variegata'

Aubretia 'Greencourt Purple'

Rhodanthemum hosmariense

Saxifraga × arendsii 'Ingeborg'

Aubretia 'Red Carpet'

Aubretia 'Wanda'

Armeria juniperifolia × maritima

Ranunculus montana 'Molten Lava'

Trifolium repens 'Purpurascens'

Saxifraga moschata 'Cloth of Gold'

Aubretia 'Aureovariegata'

A rock garden in a raised bed

Skill level:

Some experience of

growing alpines

Best time to do:

Early to late spring

Special tools required:

Narrow planting

trowel. A border spade

Time required:

Probably an entire

weekend

WHAT YOU WILL NEED

• Selection of alpines (pre-soaked)
• Gravel and broken rocks or slate shards for surface drainage
• General digging tools
• Narrow planting trowel
• Gritty alpine grit for decorative top dressing
• A few well-chosen rocks

Rock gardens made in raised beds offer well-drained conditions for alpines and bring these dainty plants closer to eye level. Use railway sleepers or decorative building blocks to make a low retaining wall. A thick layer of gravel and broken rocks on the surface of the bed allows fleshy plants to rest on a fast-drying surface to avoid rotting, and a high proportion of gravel in the soil beneath means that surface water runs away fast. The ideal rock garden soil is well drained yet moisture retentive. This is easily achieved by mixing topsoil, gritty sand and gravel, and a low-nutrient form of organic matter (such as peat or coir) in roughly equal quantities. Plant rock plants in early spring to give them some time to establish before summer sun dries out the top of the bed too much. However, plants can be put in even when in flower, provided you water them for the first few months. Relatively few rock plants tolerate searing hot sun all day – most prefer a situation that gives them a few hours of shade cast by nearby rocks or bigger plants.

Viola 'Molly Sanderson'

Silene 'Druett's Variegated'

Aubretia 'Blue Down'

Saxifraga 'Fleece'

Arabis fernandii-coburgii 'Variegata'

Aubretia 'Red Carpet'

Aubretia 'Blue Mist'

Saxifraga 'Cloth of Gold'

Primula auricula

Saxifraga 'Silver Cushion'

Oxalis adenophylla

Raoulia australis

Saxifraga cotyledon 'Southside Seedling'

Saxifraga 'Finding'

Sempervivum 'Commander Hay'

Saxifraga 'Peter Pan'

Saxifraga aizoon 'Balcana'

Arenaria balearica

Aubretia 'Astola'

1 Before adding a new plant to a bed, scrape away the gritty topdressing from the planting site using a narrow-bladed trowel. Dig a hole slightly larger than the pot containing the new plant.

2 Knock the plant out of its pot and plant it. Break up the soil at the base of the hole so that new roots can grow into the ground.

3 Replace the gritty topdressing around the plant. Leave an area of clear gravel around distinct groups of plants to show them off.

ALPINES IN TERRACOTTA POTS

If you do not have room for a complete rock garden, as an alternative you can grow many alpines in terracotta pots or pans. This keeps your collection portable if you enjoy re-organising the display from time to time. Also, some alpines need to be kept away from winter wet though they are perfectly hardy and the advantage of planting in portable pots is that you can transfer them quite easily to a cold frame or cold greenhouse with staging when conditions change suddenly.

above: These shallow terracotta pots contain a wonderful array of houseleeks (Sempervivum). Pots are a wonderful way of displaying a collection of the same genus, but try mixed selections, too.

1 Crock the base to stop soil escaping. Half-fill the pot with alpine potting mix and to give the impression of a specimen, plant three rooted cuttings together.

2 Firm the plants in gently and interweave the stems slightly so that they look more like a single plant. The plant used in this demonstration is *Erodium trifolium*.

Making a herb garden

Versatile Herbs

Herbs earn their keep in any garden, adding fragrance, culinary value and colourful foliage and flowers, as well as attracting butterflies and bees. Plant them in formal geometric beds, flower borders or containers for all-round ambience and old-fashioned 'cottage' appeal.

Related Projects

- **Simple classical topiary with box pp 58–59**
- **Laying paving slabs on sand pp 74–75**
- **How to lay block pavers pp 76–79**
- **Thyme path pg 99**
- **Installing a fountain pg 214**
- **Making a feature with climbing roses pp 138–139**
- **Making a window box pp 184–185**
- **Small formal pools pp 192–193**
- **Woven willow effects pp 232–233**
- **Building garden seating pp 240–241**

Half the fun of growing a herb collection is choosing and creating the garden or feature they are to make. If you just want a few culinary varieties within easy reach of the back door or have only very limited space, grow a selection of herbs in containers or in a bed with various easy-to-grow vegetables. Other people want to grow as many different types as they can find, in a semi-organised profusion of scents and colours. The informal herb garden may look a bit wild, but it is laid out to quite a strict plan. This type of garden suits a large plot, but can be adapted to a small garden, even though many traditional herbs including mints and lemon balm are quite invasive. If you prefer a formal style, bear in mind that many shrubby herbs such as rosemary, santolina and lavender can be clipped into formal shapes and low hedges. The wide variety of leaf shapes and sizes makes herbs ideal for providing contrasting clumps of colour within an intricate knot design or formal pattern laid out with bricks or paving. The actual herbs you choose will be highly personal too; you might treat them simply as ornamental and aromatic garden plants; select your favourite herbs for cooking; or perhaps make a selection of medicinal species or useful dye plants.

*Variegated lemon balm (*Melissa officinalis *'Aurea')*

Golden marjoram (Origanum vulgare *'Aureum'*)

Flat leaved parsley (Petroselinum crispum neapolitanum)

Marjoram (Origanum vulgare)

Ginger mint (Mentha × gracilis *'Variegata')*

Bay (Laurus nobilis)

Common thyme (Thymus vulgaris)   *Purple sage* (Salvia officinalis *'Purpurasecens')*   *Thymus* 'Silver Pride'

A DISPLAY OF MINT

An ingenious way of growing a collection of mints is to plant them in a variety of terracotta pots of different sizes, thus displaying their range of colour, shape and texture. The mints included here are: spicy ginger mint, variegated apple mint, pennyroyal, peppermint, spearmint and red raripila.

Creeping forms of pennyroyal make a scented carpet of small leaves. This is not an edible herb.

left: *This informal herb garden uses a wonderful mixture of culinary as well as purely decorative herbs. It will look quite bare when many of the plants have died down for winter but the potted bay tree and decorative surfacing will prevent the area from losing all its visual interest.*

A chessboard display

Skill level:

Beginner gardener

Best time to do:

Late spring

Special tools required:

Garden rake, shovel,

bricklayer's trowel,

secateurs, hand trowel

Time required:

Depending on the scale,

up to a day once all

materials are to hand

WHAT YOU WILL NEED

• Assorted low growing and spreading herbs
• Specimen for pot in centre
• Terracotta pot
• 4 box plants to clip to shape
• Gravel
• Paving slabs
• Bricks for edging
• Wooden batten
• Bricklayer's trowel, garden rake, shovel, secateurs, hand trowel

This contemporary version of a traditional geometric herb garden is more in keeping with the style of a modern home, and can be adapted for a space of any shape or size. It is based on the alternate black and white squares of a chessboard and could easily be created in the corner of a large patio by removing some of the slabs and improving the soil underneath. It would make a good form of flooring for a small fragrant courtyard garden, but could also become an attractive herb feature in a family garden, especially if linked with a seat and taller potted herbs. The combination of herbs and paving is a particularly effective one, since the paving reflects heat and light, which provide ideal growing conditions for the plants. In this situation, herbs produce more concentrated essential oils, which in turn perfume the air, especially when the plants are crushed as you step on odd sprigs overhanging the paving. The most suitable species to use are the more decorative but naturally compact bushy herbs that will not get overgrown quickly, such as purple sage, double flowered Roman chamomile, purple basil, orange thyme, and pineapple sage.

1 Herbs need good drainage; on heavy soil spread 2.5-5cm (1-2in) of grit or gravel over the planting area and dig in. Remove weeds and debris and rake level. Shovel gravel onto the areas where the paving slabs are to go. Compact the soil down first by treading it well with your feet.

2 Sit the paving slabs in place so that alternate slabs and soil make a pattern like the black and white squares on a chessboard. Wriggle the slabs down into their gravel bases as you lay them, so they are firmly bedded down and will not move later once you start walking on them.

3 Surround the feature with contrasting bricks laid on their narrowest edge and sunk to about half their depth into the soil. This is enough to hold them firmly. Tap down each brick as it is laid, using the handle of the trowel. Dig out a flat bottomed 'bed' for each brick so that they are even and stable.

SUITABLE PLANTS
Most non-invasive Mediterranean-style herbs that like well-drained soil and sun will thrive in a bed like this. Choose the most decorative of the low-growing bushy kinds or creeping varieties. Good ones include purple sage, gold-variegated sage, golden marjoram, or prostrate rosemary. Choose well-scented kinds and/or those with good flowers for the container in the middle; a French lavender like 'Papillon', a frilly-leaved variety of basil such as 'Purple Ruffles', an upright rosemary, pineapple sage, or a trimmed bay tree would all be ideal for such a situation.

4 Plant up the soil squares. This formal bed resembles those of a historic geometric herb garden, but on a scale in keeping with today's modern gardens. Choose low spreading herbs for this style of bed, as they will billow out over the slabs, releasing their scents when they are crushed. Take the pots off before planting and avoid breaking up the rootball.

5 A small sphere-trained box tree in each corner suits the formal style. This gold-variegated box is slower-growing than the green forms, but looks more distinctive. Snip off the tips of any long shoots.

6 Spread a 2.5-5cm(1-2in) layer of gravel over the surface as a mulch. These pink granite chippings set off the plants and tone in with the brick surround.

Dwarf lavender '*Munstead*'

Thymus serpyllum (wild thyme)

7 A decorative terracotta urn with lavender makes a good centrepiece. A feature like this could be inset into a patio or lawn, and would make a perfect focal point for a small enclosed 'garden room'.

Origanum vulgare 'Gold Tip' (marjoram)

Sanguisorba minor (salad burnet)

Chamaemelum '*Treneague*', *a non-flowering variety.*

Buxus sempervirens '*Aureovariegata*'. *Clip once a year, in late summer, to maintain its shape.*

Lining a path with a lavender hedge

Skill level:

Gardener with some

propagation experience

Best time to do:

Summer

Special tools required:

None

Time required:

Cuttings take a couple

of hours to organise

and plants will be

ready in 8–10 weeks

WHAT YOU WILL NEED

• A well grown dwarf lavender
plant
• Sharp scissors
• 9cm pots
• Gritty seed mixture
• Straightedge or taught line to
plant against
• Hand trowel

Dwarf hedges are a good way to divide up the interior of a small garden into compartments, without creating a lot of shade or taking up much room. Since a dwarf hedge is 30cm(12in) tall at most, it also makes the perfect edge for a formal flower bed, knot garden or traditional, geometric herb bed. The idea here is to outline beds, paths and borders with a continuous row of plants, clipped hedge-fashion. Team them with small topiary box balls, to add architectural detail to the ends of rows or at corners. The best plants for dwarf edgings are naturally upright, evergreen kinds that can be clipped to keep them to the required size and shape. Dwarf box (*Buxus microphylla* 'Faulkner') is ideal for a foliage hedge, but if you want something with flowers or that is a little less formal, try lavender. There are several dwarf kinds available, including the familiar 'Munstead' (easily grown from seed or cuttings) and 'Hidcote'. The grey-green foliage is particularly silvery at certain times of year, the flowers are long-lasting and release a wonderful aroma on hot days and bees and butterflies love them!

1 In summer, choose strong, non-flowering shoots 5-7.5cm(2-3in) long to make cuttings. Take them from a lavender plant in the garden, or buy one plant from a nursery. Strip off the lower leaves by running your thumb and finger down the stem. Leave about four full-sized leaves at the tip.

2 Nip out the growing tip using your finger and thumbnail. This helps to produce a bushy plant. Hedging plants must branch from the base to avoid a gappy effect. Make a clean cut just below the bottom leaf joint, which can be seen as a scar on the stalk. This removes any tissue that might rot, causing the cutting to die.

3 Prepare all your cuttings at once. Take about 30% more than you need to allow for failures. You can also then select only the best for planting later. Push each cutting individually into a small pot filled with seed mix. Water the cuttings well and stand them in a sheltered spot out of direct sunlight. Check the cuttings daily.

4 Eight to ten weeks after taking the cuttings, you should have many young plants with plenty of vigorous branching shoots that are just beginning to flower. The pots will be filled with roots and are ready for planting.

5 Now prepare the soil for planting and mark out the row. Tap down the pots to loosen the plants and knock out the cuttings without disturbing the rootball. Plant them firmly, about 15cm (6in) apart. Straight after planting, cut the plants back by a third to a half. This reduces water loss and encourages branching.

above: *A dwarf lavender hedge is reminiscent of cottage gardens. Trim with small shears annually, immediately after flowers have faded, clipping off the tops of the newest shoots. This promotes bushiness. Cutting hard back may kill the plant.*

left: *Choose young plants of a similar size and the same variety. Plant them into a light, well-drained soil every 50cm(20in). Allow each plant to spread itself a little as it settles into position. A little bark mulch will keep down weeds. Water the plants in well.*

A ROSEMARY HEDGE

Rosemary will make a somewhat taller hedge than lavender growing to around 4ft (1.2m) and is just as easy to grow given a sunny well-drained spot. It releases its fragrant oil into the atmosphere at the slightest touch and is therefore ideal as an informal hedge running alongside a path or bordering an outdoor dining area. Choose the variety 'Miss Jessopp's Upright'.

Herbs in containers

WHAT YOU WILL NEED

• A selection of herbs chosen for compatibility and to create a pleasing combination of colour, texture and form
• A terracotta trough
• Crocks and gravel for drainage
• Gritty, soil-based potting mix
• Narrow planting trowel
• Fine decorative gravel as a mulch

A trough or windowbox is the perfect way to grow a selection of culinary herbs in the minimum of space. The kitchen windowsill is an obvious site, providing the window opens conveniently enough for regular access to your mini-garden. Make sure that the windowbox is firmly secured; use strong brackets or ties and check these periodically for wear or weathering. The box might be home-made from new or old timber, painted to match window frames or shutters; or it might be lightweight plastic, antique stone or terracotta. If the windows provide too exposed a site, why not plant up an indoor windowbox, perfect for a few of the more tender species, such as basil. Regular cropping or trimming is important to ensure that the herbs remain small and leafy. Keep the box adequately watered and apply a liquid feed during the growing and cropping season to replace essential nutrients. A mulch of small pebbles helps to conserve moisture.

THE VERSATILITY OF HERBS IN CONTAINERS

Herbs look great in pots; you can group them in large containers or grow them in individual pots on walls, patios, decks, balconies or terraces. They are also ideal for small garden areas: not only are they edible, they also produce a prolonged, attractive display and scent the area, too. This in turn will attract butterflies and bees. Choosing the right blend of herbs for your containers can be great fun. Even taking into account soil compatibility and whether the plants need sun or shade, there is plenty of scope to create pleasing contrasts of colour, from darkest green to fresh lime; of foliage, from broadleaved to spiky or fleshy; and of size, from tall to tiny trailing varieties.

1 Choose a selection of herbs with a variety of foliage shapes and textures. Place a few crocks in the bottom of the trough. Add a 5-15cm(2-6in) layer of washed gravel or pea shingle to make a well-draining layer at the bottom. Top up with planting mix.

2 Plant the herbs, maintaining a pleasing balance of appearance, height and habit. Tip them gently out of their pots and into your hand, supporting the rootball lightly between your fingers.

COLOURFUL HERBS IN WICKER

Massed together, herbs tend to look predominantly green, so you need to mix in varieties with contrasting leaf textures and colours. A temporary display of young herbs can be made by disguising the pots with a surround of woven willow or crumbling old bricks, both of which have a suitably organic, country or cottage garden look. For a more permanent display, plant up a lined wicker basket.

3 Top up with soil, making sure it settles between the plants without any air gaps. To allow for watering, do not fill to the top of the box.

4 A sprinkling of gravel or small stones on top of the soil around the plants not only looks attractive, but also helps to slow down moisture loss.

Sage
(Salvia officinalis)

Chives
(Allium schoenoprasum)

Sorrel (Rumex acetosa)

Parsley
(Petroselinum
crispum)

Oregano
(Origanum
vulgare)

Culinary thyme (Thymus vulgaris)

French tarragon (Artemisia dracunculus)

A classical garden

Plant Associations

Team pink/orange-tinged birch trunks (Betula albo-sinensis and B. utilis) with pieris or rhododendron. Craggy pine trunks team well with golden bushy conifers. Acer trunks with red dogwood stems stand out brilliantly in front of blue conifers in winter. Conifers and heathers are a classic combination.

Related Projects

- **Terracotta tiles and edges pg 83**
- **Making a feature of your lawn pp 88–91; Lawn edging pp 94–95**
- **Overhead structures in the garden pp 124–125**
- **Planting a clematis obelisk pp 132–133**
- **Erecting a pergola pp 146–147**
- **A classic urn for autumn pp 164–165**
- **Small formal pools pp 192–193**
- **Installing fountains pg 214**
- **Garden illusions and effects with mirrors pp 244–245**

The formal garden is characterised by its strong, architectural lines. There are clipped hedges and other kinds of framework planting, straight pathways leading purposefully to focal points – a stone statue, a fountain – and evergreens creating an atmosphere of timelessness. You don't have to own a mansion to have a garden with classical styling – in fact the formal garden works beautifully in a small space and can be adapted to suit modern or period architecture. Use evergreen hedges and decorative trelliswork to create intimate garden areas and a feeling of enclosure and seclusion. Lay out brick or gravel paths connecting to simple geometric shapes – circles, squares and rectangles and create mini vistas through archways and gaps in hedging. One or two carefully arranged focal points such as a wooden bench seat, wall fountain or stone urn will draw the eye and help to make the garden a serene and tranquil place. Select compact evergreen shrubs and ground cover plants to form the foundation of the borders. And keep this planting as varied as possible by making full use of foliage colour, shape and texture. Add climbers such as white rambler roses and wisteria and soft-coloured herbaceous.

right: *Topiary is a standard feature of the classical garden. It does not all take years to grow – this little ivy spiral would only take a few months.*

right: *Formal box hedges and stone ornaments are quintessential elements of a classical garden which do not always need a large area in which to work well.*

Seasonal Effect

The non-evergreens in a garden like this need to work hard, without making hard work. Choose bulbs of the type that can be left permanently naturalised between shrubs, including a mixture of dwarf spring bulbs (which do not have obtrusive foliage that makes the garden look untidy for weeks after the flowers are over), summer bulbs such as lilies, and autumn bulbs such as colchicum. Also add some perennials that look good over a long season but will not need dividing frequently, such as hostas, euphorbia, hardy ferns, Acanthus spinosus and perennial grasses. Where possible, also use compact or ground-covering evergreens.

Variegated evergreens *Make the most of variegated evergreens such as euonymus and hebe to 'lift' a collection of evergreen shrubs. There are plants with shades of cream, gold, silver, lime and lemon in their leaves, and a wide range of markings, including speckles, dapples, blotches, splashes and neat edgings to the leaves. This is* Hebe × franciscana *'Variegata'.*

Coloured evergreens *The* Choisya ternata *'Sundance' shown here and other coloured foliage evergreens are specially valuable for adding variety to what could easily become a sea of very similar-looking shades of green.*

Architectural plants *Bold, architecturally-shaped plants, such as this* Mahonia × media *'Buckland', provide the structure of the garden. Like sculptures, do not overdo them.*

Euonymus fortunei 'Emerald Gaiety'

Carex conica 'Hime-kan-suge' ('Snowline')

Bricks and statues *In a small garden, it is important that all the 'hard' ingredients have something in common. Here, both the bricks and the statue are terracotta.*

Hedera helix (ivy)

Ajuga reptans 'Braunherz'

Hedera helix (ivy)

Santolina chamaecyparissus nana

Classic features

Living Focal Points

In the classical garden you can use clipped and trained plants in place of conventional garden ornaments, provided they are symmetrically placed and given sufficient prominence. Simple geometric topiary designs work well, as do small weeping trees, and plants with a strikingly architectural form.

The secret to success for creating the elegant formal garden look is restraint. It is worth saving up to buy just one or two really nice pieces but you don't have to spend a lot or go for the genuine antiques. It is quite easy to fool people with concrete and reconstituted stone reproductions and you can now buy very convincing copies of stoneware and large terracotta jars made from plastic. The only problem with brand-new pieces is that they are often very bright and unblemished. But you can soften, age and generally dull down a piece with acrylic paints applied with a natural sponge to give the stippled effect of algae or brush darker colours into crevices and contours. Look out for stone and terracotta wall masks featuring characters from mythology and set them, half-hidden by climbers for an air of mystery. A simple wooden armchair would make an excellent focal point at the end of a pathway, but don't forget to give yourself something to look at when you are sitting in it! There's a lot of theatre in the placing of garden ornaments, and the position you give an object together with its backdrop can make all the difference. For example a gothic metalwork seat or a bust on a plinth could be given pride of place by standing it at the end of a walkway, or beneath a simple wire archway. These can be bought in easy-to-assemble packs from the garden centre. Use a quick growing climber such as a rambler rose, honeysuckle or jasmine, to camouflage it in no time. Shaped trellis panels that trick the eye by creating false perspective are called *trompe l'oeil* features and work well in the classical garden making wonderful set pieces, as the photo left illustrates admirably well.

left: *This photograph illustrates some of the dramatic touches used to create a really eye-catching focal point. A large pot is the centrepiece, symmetrically framed by an imaginary 'archway' of trellis, the 3-D effect emphasised by the arc of climbers. Planting at the base completes the framing.*

left: *The original of this classically inspired ornament would be prohibitively expensive. Brand new, the reproductions look rather raw but mellow once weathered to become convincing look-alikes.*

right: *The stylised peacock with its fantail is a traditional design for topiary and one that is surprisingly easy to clip using either box or yew. You can either buy wire frames to guide your clipping or work freehand and by eye.*

Do:

• Plan the garden using simple geometric shapes and straight paths

• Use traditional elements for paving such as terracotta, stone and gravel

• Create focal points and vistas using formally trained plants and classically inspired garden ornaments

• Concentrate on evergreen shrubs and ground cover plants to generate a timeless atmosphere

Don't:

• Reject reproduction ornaments and fake terracotta. With some simple paint effects and proper siting, these can look very convincing

• Forget the need for seasonal changes. Incorporate some deciduous trees and shrubs, herbaceous perennials and bulbs

• Create too many 'features' otherwise the atmosphere will become too 'busy'

Simple classical topiary with box

Skill level:

Beginner gardener: it

may look difficult, but

it isn't!

Best time to do:

Summer to early

autumn

Special tools required:

Secateurs, sheep

shears, 'ladies' shears

Time required:

Varies according to size

WHAT YOU WILL NEED

• Box cutting or bushy, rounded plant that hasn't yet been properly shaped.
• Pots to pot on into as the plant grows plus fresh compost
• Secateurs
• One-handed shears, sheep shears or 'ladies' shears
• Lined terracotta pot to display the finished topiary

Box (Buxus sempervirens) is one of the most popular topiary plants because it responds well to clipping and can be used to create quite complex shapes with fine detail. It is very 'tolerant' but it grows much more strongly and healthily given the right conditions – light shade, moisture-retentive soil rich in organic matter, a mulch to keep surface roots cool, and a buoyant atmosphere to discourage disease. Clipping forces the plant to create more and more shoots at the branch tips leading to congestion. This causes the leaves within the outer 'skin' of dense foliage to die off. So every few years, open up the plant by removing a few whole branches to let in more light and air. Clean out debris that accumulates within the plant as well as dead leaves and clippings from the ground. Box topiary can be grown permanently in large containers, ideally wider than deep to accommodate its surface-roots. Line terracotta with plastic to prevent moisture loss or use glazed pots. You can shape existing bushes into a dome or sphere by clipping with shears. But for more complicated shapes such as ball-headed standards, cones, spirals or animals, start with a very small plant, or a rooted cutting. Take these during late spring and summer. Snip 7.5cm (3in) pieces from the tips of the shoots and remove the lower leaves. Push them to two-thirds their length into pots or trays of seed mix and keep moist and shady. When rooted – after six to eight weeks – pot each cutting into a 10cm(4in) pot and pinch out the growing tip to make it bushy.

GROWING A BOX BALL

Start with a single strong cutting or young plant – you can sometimes pick these up as hedging and they are much cheaper than plants sold for topiary. Avoid the dwarf form, *Buxus sempervirens* 'Suffruticosa', as this will take a long time to grow to any size. Begin training by nipping out shoots with thumb and forefinger, progress to secateurs, then use shears to create a smooth globe shape. One handed shears or sheep shears are okay for small pieces, but a pair of small, 'ladies' shears are ideal for general trimming and a lot less tiring.

1 Start with a strong, rooted box cutting. Nip off the growing tips of the shoots using forefinger and thumbnail. Repeat when the side shoots are 2.5cm(1in) long.

2 Use secateurs to nip back the tips of the next crop of side shoots. Each time new growth reaches 5cm(2in) long, shorten it. Pruning encourages bushiness.

3 As the first pot fills with roots, move the plant into a larger pot with fresh potting mixture. Clip the plant regularly using small shears instead of secateurs.

4 When it reaches the required size, just snip off any errant shoots that appear during the year and from then on clip lightly once a year in late summer.

A BOX HEDGE

Box hedging is very much part of the mental picture we create when we think of formal gardens. It looks very smart clipped with architectural precision. Box is normally used to make a relatively low hedge compared to yew, but if you want a really tiny hedge to create a formal edging for borders or the pattern of knot gardens and parterres, use the dwarf 'Suffruticosa' or *Buxus microphylla* 'Faulkner'.

5 Your topiary will continue to grow and it is a mistake to try to keep it exactly the same size for very long. However, do perfect the shape over time.

6 It is possible to create a good box ball about 23cm (9in) across by this method in three years. Plant in the ground or pot into lined terracotta.

above: *A low box hedge lines the gravel path leading to an alcove of yew that surrounds a small statue. Notice how the ends of the hedge have been clipped into spheres mirroring the architectural form of stonework; in fact, it would be fair to say that clipped hedging really is a form of green architecture.*

Quick and easy potted topiary

Classic topiary shapes include domes, cones, globes and spirals, right through to more fanciful shapes, such as peacocks and teapots. On a small scale, geometric forms and many of the shapes currently in fashion, such as teddy bears, are suitable for growing in pots. Box, *Ligustrum delavayanum*, holly, bay and *Ilex crenata*, will all tolerate being containerised, but avoid yew which can suffer if grown in pots long-term. They all withstand clipping and their dense evergreen foliage gives the shapes a solid, architectural feel. For really speedy results try the shrubby honeysuckle, *Lonicera nitida*, which has very fine leaves and is often grown as a quick hedge. The only disadvantage is that unlike classic topiary subjects it requires frequent clipping to keep it in shape and is not as long-lived. Not all shapes need a frame, for example domes and globes, and as you become more confident you might try one or two shapes freehand, such as cones and spirals. But larger garden centres now sell basic frames in plastic-coated wire, as well as trellis obelisks in wood or plastic. The latter sit over the top of the plant and you simply trim any growth that pushes through the gaps.

1 Transfer a suitable plant to a large ornamental container. This fast-growing shrub is *Lonicera nitida* 'Baggesen's Gold'. Sit the plant in the centre of the pot. Fill in round the root-ball with potting mix.

2 Gather the stems loosely and fit the frame over the top. With all the stems inside, press the cone gently into the mix until it is stable.

3 Tuck any stray shoots behind the wires. This thickens up the shape and ensures that protruding stems will not be snipped off. Working all round the plant, secure strong upright stems to the frame with ties. This makes the shape more solid right away.

4 Snip off any protruding straggly shoots. Remove the very tips of thin straight shoots to encourage them to branch out. The cone is taking shape.

5 *Lonicera nitida* soon fills out the frame. When horizontal side shoots start to make the outline look rather shaggy, the plant is ready for its final shaping.

6 Tie a string to the base of the frame. Sweep the stems up with one hand and bind them in place with the other. Do not cut them off; they fill out the shape.

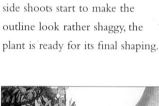

7 At the top, tie the string firmly to the frame. Snip off any protruding stems, leaving the cone with a neatly pointed tip.

8 Sheep shears are ideal for trimming off any stems that stick out from the sides of the cone, leaving the shape tidy.

The finished cone has taken less than three months to complete. It will need clipping every few weeks from spring to autumn.

VARIATIONS ON A THEME

Box spirals can be cut instantly from a bushy, cone-shaped plant with a single main stem. As you form the spiral, you cut into the plant, and if there are several main stems coming from the base, you risk creating a large hole. Tie a piece of string round the rim of the pot and wind it around the cone creating a marker for the spiral groove. Tie off at the top and then use secateurs to cut a V-shaped mark that follows the string. Remove the string and then continue clipping with small shears. Keep the spirals neat and tidy by trimming them regularly.

Paths and Paving

One of the first things to do when laying out a new garden is to mark the lines of pathways and hard surfaces throughout the space. This will give you a strong groundplan that will hold the design together even if the plantings grow to be especially exuberant. There are endless possibilities when it comes to the fabric of paths and paving that you could choose for your garden, and their importance as a decorative element should not be overlooked. In the following pages, we will consider several easy but attractive options for a variety of different garden floors. Of course, hard landscaping can be expensive, depending on the materials you choose, but you can always surface with something relatively cheap such as gravel until your budget will stretch. There are many attractive options to consider.

Design tips for paths

Everyday use: Paths that take you where you need to go – to the garage, a gate or a washing line – should go as straight as possible, otherwise people will cut corners and walk over the flower beds.

Heavy use: Paths that carry heavy weights, such as vehicles, need to be wide enough and have deeper foundations than those that will only be walked on.

Scenic routes: Paths intended to encourage meandering round the garden should twist and curve to slow you down and open up new vistas at each turn. They can be narrow, decorated by containers, or lead to seats, arbours or dead ends. They need little or no foundations as they will not have to carry weight.

Levels: Use paths and walkways to create the appearance of changing levels. Make 'bridges' over beds of plants, a pond, bog garden or even plain gravel. Or set railway sleepers into the ground at an angle with gravel between them to 'suggest' steps.

Textures: Use paths and paving to create different textures and to contrast with planting. Don't be afraid to mix and match.

An essential item of the garden is some form of access that remains reasonably dry and safe underfoot in all weathers and allows you to move from one feature to another. Without it, you will create unsightly tracks. But walkways, paths and stepping stones have important design possibilities, too. They can be strictly formal making geometric shapes, or they can meander between features, creating a more relaxed feel. Because the eye naturally follows the shape and line of any pathway into the distance and beyond, the path can influence the appearance and shape of the site visually. Take it straight from A to B and the plot seems shorter, but describe a more circuitous route

and the garden instantly appears bigger and more interesting, especially if you cannot see right to the end. If a solid path seems too dominant, use stepping stones or a staggered wooden walkway. The materials you use will influence the look and feel of your garden; stone slabs and pavers can be adapted to both formal and informal schemes. For a cottage garden style, lay brick in ornamental herringbone patterns, or for a woodland feel, lay a path of wood chips with log slices as stepping stones. To soften the effect of paths and walkways, encourage them to blend into the general garden scheme. Let plants spill over the edge; low-growing, carpet-forming prostrate plants, such as creeping

Do:

• Mark out the line of paths first with wooden pegs or six inch nails and walk them to get a feel
• Make pathways wide enough, allowing room for plants to spill over the edges
• Get samples of bricks and paving to test out before you buy
• Consider hiring a cement mixer
• Shop around for well-priced materials

Don't:

• Skimp on quality. If you can't afford the paving of your choice, Use cheaper materials like gravel or bark as a temporary measure
• Ignore the need for proper preparation
• Try to do too much at once. Paving slabs can be very heavy and accidents and injuries tend to happen when you get tired!

opposite page: *This highly formal layout with wide gravel paths laid in a geometric form gives strength to the design yet allows the planting to relaxed and carefree.*

right: *This shallow flight of steps with sawn wooden risers infilled with light-coloured stone chippings gives the garden a sunny Mediterranean feel. Logs and bark would be more informal.*

thyme, are also useful for growing between the pavers or bricks of a path. Or position pots of plants along the route to soften the hard edges and sharp corners.

If you are stuck with ugly cracked or uneven paving in your garden, perhaps laid by a previous occupant, do not despair. Replacing the surface with fresh paving slabs, gravel or even brick is relatively easy when you re-use the underlying foundations. And if an area of paving feels too big and maybe somewhat boring as a result, just lift a few slabs and either replace them with smaller units like bricks or cobbles or fill the vacant spaces with planting. There are plenty of ideas in the pages to come.

Making a gravel path

Skill level:

DIY experience useful

Best time to do:

Anytime the ground is

dry and not frozen

Special tools required:

Garden roller; garden

rake; shovel; mallet;

hammer; saw

Time required:

One to two days'

labour time

WHAT YOU WILL NEED

• Lengths of preservative treated wood to cut into pegs
• Preservative-treated gravel boards
• Galvanised nails
• Crushed rock or fine hardcore
• Gravel or stone chippings
• Semi-permeable membrane (optional)
• Mallet, hammer, roller, shovel and garden rake

A path or other gravel area can be an attractive feature in any garden, especially when used to provide contrast alongside flat paving materials and low-growing plants. Areas of gravel are also a particularly popular feature of oriental-style gardens. True gravel is available in a range of mixed natural-earth shades that look particularly good when wet, while crushed stone, which is rough-edged rather than smooth, is sold in a range of colours from white through reds and greens to grey and black. Although both are attractive and are relatively inexpensive to lay, they do have several practical drawbacks. They need a solid edge to prevent stones from straying onto lawns and flowerbeds. They may also need weeding fairly regularly if you don't use a semi-permeable membrane to separate the gravel from the soil below. Avoid fine gravel which may be viewed by cats as an ideal earth closet!

1 Excavate the area over which you want to lay the gravel until you reach solid subsoil. Set out preservative-treated boards around the perimeter of the excavated area.

2 Secure the boards to the pegs with galvanised nails. Add more pegs at roughly 1m(39in) intervals along the boards all round the area to prevent the boards from bowing.

3 The best way of discouraging weeds from growing up through a gravel path is to put down a porous membrane.

4 To form a firm base for the gravel, cover the membrane with a layer of crushed rock or fine hardcore. You will need at least 50mm(2in) of rock on firm subsoil, and more if it is soft.

5 Compact the base layer by running a heavy garden roller over it. Fill in any hollows and roll it again until you no longer leave any footprints in the surface. Thorough preparation prevents sinking in the future. Without disturbing the base layer, spread out the gravel or decorative stone. Fill the area up to the level of the perimeter boards.

6 Level the gravel. Draw a wooden straightedge along the tops of the boards to identify high spots or hollows. Rake again.

VARIATIONS ON THE THEME

Bags of slate shards are now available from the garden centre as well as builder's merchants and DIY stores. They make a very attractive and unusual surfacing alternative to gravel. They complement planting perfectly and work particularly well in Japanese-style gardens. But you can also incorporate them into cottage schemes like the one above and use them to make rough tracks in wild and woodland gardens. The shards can have sharp edges, so keep children away from them.

Flair with decorative edgings

Skill level:

Some experience with

powered cutting tools

valuable

Best time to do:

Anytime the ground is

not too wet or frozen

Special tools required:

Tile cutter; garden rake

Time required:

Up to a day, depending

on the length of path

WHAT YOU WILL NEED

• Pantiles
• Diamond cutter
• Gravel
• Garden rake
• Semi-permeable membrane
(optional)
• Fine hardcore

Straight gravel boards are relatively inexpensive and quick and easy to install but if you want to upgrade your gravel paths and give them a decorative finish, why not choose an alternative path edging. Bricks are ideal for curving paths and for creating circular planting features within gravel. If you can get hold of them, clay pantiles, normally used for roofing, also look well with gravel. Old bricks laid on the diagonal would be perfect for creating the country house or cottage garden look. In a Victorian or Edwardian style setting, choose a barley twist or rope edging or edging tiles with shaped tops. Low log roll could be pegged in place just like gravel boards but has the advantage of being able to go round curves. Use it in a wild or woodland garden. Whatever edging you choose, it should come a little way above the surface of the gravel to keep the stones in place.

above: *Old bricks set into the ground on the diagonal form a not too perfect edging that adds just the right note to this relaxed cottage-style planting. Save work in the form of weeding by not growing prolific self-seeders like* Alchemilla mollis *next to gravel paths.*

1 Cut each pantile in half and bed the pieces into the soil, so that they overlap and the curves fit into each other, leaning slightly outwards.

2 Leave 7.5cm (3in) of the tile edges standing above soil level. Support them evenly on both sides and tread down gently to secure them.

3 When the entire surface of the path is firmed down, spread a layer of shingle, rake it lightly and tread it up against the tile faces.

COPING WITH A GRADIENT

Use rows of brick pavers, railway sleepers or stone setts partly sunk into the ground to convert a slightly sloping path into a series of long shallow steps. They also prevent rain washing the gravel downhill. Make sure the bricks are firmly fixed. You can also buy mini-sleepers which are easy to handle and to cut to length. Just use heavy wooden pegs to hold them in position. Rustic logs, still with the bark on, can be fixed in the same way and suit the wild or woodland garden.

above : *Make a narrow trench with a spade and sink in the rope-edged tiles. Back fill with gravel. You can now edge the lawn with a strimmer.*

above: *An attractive, old-fashioned, jagged brick edge looks good in a cottage garden or vegetable plot. You can use either new or secondhand bricks.*

ALTERNATIVE EDGINGS

As well as ready-made edgings available from the garden centre, you can also create your own, using rough quarried stone such as slabs of slate standing on edge and set into concrete foundations. You could also use large pieces of dressed stone or heavy logs which still have their bark on, for example silver birch tree branches, which will not require foundations.

Cultivating an informal look

Skill level:

DIY experience useful

Best time to do:

Anytime the ground is

not too wet or frozen

Special tools required:

Hammer; mallet; spade;

spirit level

Time required:

One to two days,

although this depends

on the size of the area

to be worked on

WHAT YOU WILL NEED

- String and pegs
- Logs cut to length
- Wooden pegs and sawn softwood edge pieces (treated with preservative)
- Sharp spade
- Mallet
- Hammer
- Galvanised nails
- Spirit level
- Topping of gravel or bark

Paths made from bricks or paving slabs are characteristically straight edged, but some gardens do not suit the formal look and many gardeners are happier with gently flowing lines. The pathway shown above, though very attractive, might actually be quite hard to maintain because the dwarf box hedge would need annual clipping – hand shears are hard to operate so close to gravel and the sharp twists and turns would make the trim even trickier. Using plants to soften the edge of a gravel path is however often a good way to introduce a more relaxed note. The glossy, large rounded leaves of elephant's ears (*Bergenia*) could for instance be planted to form a ribbon of green that lasts right through winter. A similarly striking living 'edge' could be made from *Heuchera* 'Palace Purple' (see photograph above) or a mixture of evergreen perennials, including lily turf (*Liriope muscari*). Another area in which you can introduce a more rustic feel is when making a simple flight of steps. In this case, ordinary rough sawn logs could be used.

VARIATION: SEASIDE PEBBLES

You can use all kinds of materials to make hard surfaces, especially in an informal garden. For a seaside feel, combine different sizes of pebbles and cobbles and add a touch of magic by creating 'pools' of blue or green coloured glass beads in amongst the pebbles. Never remove pebbles from beaches.

left: *Dwarf box edging holds back a froth of flowers and foliage. Box is normally a formal hedge but the zig-zag design creates a relaxed feel.*

right: *Flat rounded pebbles laid over shingle make a wonderful textural contrast with pieces of paving. Hardy herbs and alpines soften the look further.*

1 Mark out the site with pegs, string lines and one of the riser logs as a width guide. Cut away the turf from the bank between the two string lines.

2 Lay the bottom riser across the slope and secure it with two stout pegs driven vertically into the ground at each side.

4 Nail edging planks of sawn softwood to the sides of the tread. Make sure these are also treated with preservative.

3 Position the next log riser and part-drive one fixing peg. Use a batten and spirit level to position the riser accurately.

5 Peg and nail the other risers. With edging planks in position on the first tread, fill in the space with gravel or bark.

6 Complete the flight by adding edging planks to the sides of the other treads. Then fill with gravel or bark making sure it is well-compacted. Each log is positioned so that its underside is level with the top edge of the log below it, producing a shallow and easily accessible flight of steps.

Introducing pattern and texture

below: *Provided it is laid well, random stone paving can make a very attractive patterned surface, particularly around older properties or in country gardens. One advantage of this kind of paving is that, unlike rectangular paving slabs, it is very easy to work around curving or irregularly shaped features.*

Your patio or terrace can be viewed as an extension of the house. It could be used for sitting out in the sunshine, or perhaps for alfresco dining and entertaining, so why not make it special by creating a flooring that is as attractive as possible? By all means vary the texture and colouring of the patio floor to create pleasing patterns, but keep designs reasonably simple to avoid competing with the plants. In the winter especially, a decorative terrace will brighten up the outlook from the house considerably.

When choosing the various paving materials, it is always a good idea to make a visual link to the fabric of the building or to a garden wall with at least one of the paving elements, so that the design feels part of the overall scheme. Think about scale, too. In a large area you can afford to use bigger

right: *Old, reclaimed bricks (make sure they are frost proof), brick pavers or engineering bricks are small enough to be laid in a number of different patterns. They can create a very traditional or period feel in a garden as can be seen in this narrow cottage-style pathway. For extra interest, try using bands of darker or lighter brick to make contrasting borders or patterns within larger areas of paving.*

Do:

• Try to link brick pavers and other materials with the bricks used in house or boundary walls

• Work in materials used in paved areas to the fabric of raised beds, raised pools, steps and retaining walls

• Save money by surrounding areas of more expensive paving or brickwork with concrete or gravel

• Match the size of paving units to the available area

Don't:

• Leave uneven surfaces that could cause an accident

• Make designs too complex or you could make the area feel uncomfortably busy

• Forget to lay electric cable for lighting and water pipes for features like fountains before laying paving!

left: *This contemporary terrace combines brick with plain paving slabs, making a simple but highly effective geometric pattern. Notice how well the design ties in with the adjacent lawn and the pergola posts. As an alternative to the zig-zagging paved panels, you could infill with darker bricks set at an angle.*

above: *An excellent way of adding interest to a dull expanse of paving is to plant into it. All you do is lift a few slabs, dig out any cement or hardcore and replace with good quality soil. A sunny patio is naturally warmer in winter and a good place to try more tender plants and drought-loving herbs. When you have finished planting, cover the soil with a decorative mulch of gravel or small pebbles.*

paving units, but to keep things interesting provide contrasting colour and texture with blocks, bands or edgings of smaller units.

Concrete paths and drives are relatively inexpensive to create. There are firms you can hire who can colour and texture the concrete to look like brick, but you can make concrete more interesting yourself by texturing the surface before it is dry using a stiff nylon bristle brush dipped in water. Also work gravel, bits of brick and cobbles well into the surface to create the effect of a natural stone conglomerate. This is ideal for an informal garden, but for a more structured effect try edging concrete paths and patios with a wide strip of cobbles laid on end like eggs in a box, or use strips of bricks.

Laying paving slabs on sand

Skill level:

Basic DIY skills required

Best time to do:

Anytime when the

ground is not too wet

or frozen

Special tools required:

Spirit level; club

hammer; rake; shovel

Time required:

Up to a weekend,

depending on size of

area to be covered

Concrete paving is available in a wide range of 'natural' shades with riven or textured finishes that give them a softer look more suitable for the smaller garden. One of the easiest ways to pave an area is to lay small square paving slabs on a base of sand. There is no cement to mix, which keeps the job well within the capabilities of most gardeners, and if you do need to lift a slab later on, it is quite a simple task. Paving slabs measuring 45 × 45cm(18 × 18in) are relatively light and easy to handle, so most people could lay slabs of this size without assistance.

1 Unless the subsoil is firm, spread and compact a layer of solid material over the site. Excavate the site, level the subsoil and spread the hardcore.

2 Spread out the bedding sand on top of the compacted filling and rake it out evenly to a depth of 25-50mm(1-2in) across the whole site.

3 If you have edge restraints, level the sand so its surface is just less than the slab thickness below the top of the edging.

WHAT YOU WILL NEED

- 45cm(18in) square paving slabs
- Hardcore, e.g. gravel or crushed rock
- A length of fencepost to consolidate the hardcore
- Concreting sand and fine sand
- Straight edged batten
- Wooden spacers
- Gravel boards for edges
- Spirit level
- Club hammer or rubber mallet
- Garden rake, shovel and broom

4 The paving should have a slight fall (away from the house if this is adjacent) to help rainwater to run off it. Use a batten and spirit level to check the direction of the fall.

An edge restraint around the excavated site will prevent sand from leaching out.

5 Lay four slabs in one corner of the site, setting small wooden spacers between adjacent slabs to ensure an even gap for the pointing. You can remove the spacers as soon as each slab is surrounded by other slabs.

6 Lay a batten across the slabs and check the direction of the fall. If necessary, tamp the slabs further into the sand bed using the handle of a club hammer.

right: *Natural stone paving complements plants of all sorts and suits any style of garden. Use it for paths, paving and steps. It teams well with other natural hard surfaces such as gravel and cobblestones, bricks and terracotta edging stones.*

7 Continue laying slabs across the site, kneeling on a board on the sand bed if you cannot reach right across the area from the edge. Be sure to check the fall.

8 Remove the last spacers and spread some fine sand across the surface. Brush it into all the joints with a soft broom, then sweep off the excess.

How to lay block pavers

Skill level:

DIY experience required

Best time to do:

Anytime when the

ground is not too wet

or frozen

Special tools required:

Spirit level; club

hammer; rake; shovel

Time required:

Up to a weekend,

depending on size of

area to be covered

WHAT YOU WILL NEED

• Pegged gravel boards, kerbstones or path edging tiles
• Hardcore for soft ground
• A length of fence post to consolidate hardcore or subsoil
• Concreting sand and fine sand
• A straight-edged batten and spirit level
• Brick pavers
• Garden rake, shovel, club hammer or rubber mallet

Block pavers are relative newcomers to the world of garden building, but have rapidly become extremely popular because they are small and easy to handle, are designed to be dry-laid on a sand bed and need no pointing. Unlike other dry-laid paving, they can even withstand the weight of motor vehicles thanks to the way they interlock once laid, so they can be used for all hard surfaces around the garden. However, for large areas you must lay the sand bed with a continuous edge restraint to prevent the sand from leaching out. Be sure to use concreting sand for the bedding layer, as building sand is too soft and may stain the blocks. If you need to cut many blocks, hire a hydraulically operated block splitter to cut through cleanly. You can split them with a bolster chisel and club hammer, but they may not break so successfully.

1 Place edge restraints – pegged boards or kerbstones – all round the area you intend to pave. Then cover it with sand and level it roughly with a straightedge.

2 To get the blocks level with the top of the edge restraints, measure the block thickness and tamp down the sand to this depth, with a slight fall across the area.

3 Decide on the pattern you intend to follow and start placing the first blocks on the sand bed. For a path or patio tamp down with a hammer handle.

4 Most patterns have a plain border. Here, a single row is laid along each edge. Use a batten and spirit level to check that the second edge is level.

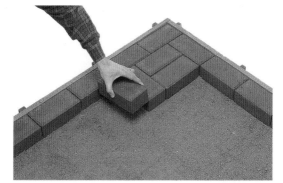

5 Start laying the blocks in your chosen pattern; this will be a simple basketweave design with pairs of blocks placed at right angles.

6 Build up the paving by adding more blocks, working away from the first corner. Check constantly that the pattern is correct as you work.

7 After completing a small area, use a straightedge to check that the blocks are level with each other.

8 Spread fine sand over the surface and brush into all the joints. Sweep off excess. Hire a plate vibrator to settle in areas of heavy usage.

Designs with pavers

Skill level:

DIY experience required

Best time to do:

Anytime when the

ground is not too wet

or frozen

Special tools required:

Club hammer, spirit

level, bolster chisel or

hired block splitter

Time required:

Up to a weekend

WHAT YOU WILL NEED

• Pegs and gravel boards as edging
• Hardcore with a length of fence post to consolidate ground
• Shovel and garden rake
• Concreting sand and fine sand
• Wooden straightedge and spirit level
• Club hammer and bolster chisel or block splitter
• Soft broom

The block paver is ideal for creating paths, patios and other paved areas in the garden, because it is light and easy to handle and quick and simple to lay. Most people choose a monochrome effect, laying pavers of just one colour and relying on the way in which they are placed for extra visual interest. However, as pavers are made to a standard size there is no reason why you should not use pavers of different colours to create distinctive patterns, or even mix them with other paving materials or cobbles. Pavers now come in a wide range of shades, from yellow and red to buff and brown and various shades of gray, so you can choose complementary or contrasting effects as you prefer. The only limit to what you can create is your own imagination.

1 A contrasting border is one of the simplest effects you can create. Here, the border pavers are laid side by side and the infill is added in herringbone style.

2 Tamp the pavers into the sand bed, using a wood offcut and a club hammer to set them level with their neighbours. Lift and relay any that sink down or stand proud.

3 Use a long wooden straightedge and a spirit level to check that there is a slight fall across the paved area. This will ensure that heavy rain can drain away freely.

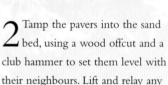

4 The continuous pattern begins to build up as you work across the area. The cut blocks at the edges of the area maintain the herringbone bond. If you have many pavers to cut hire a block splitter. Alternatively, score a cutting line deeply across its face by drawing the corner of a bolster chisel against a straightedge. Place the paver on a sand bed and cut it with a chisel and hammer.

VARIATIONS ON THE THEME

Small paving slabs or frost-proof tiles look great combined with block pavers. Choose your slabs with care so that their size coordinates with a whole number of pavers, or you will end up either with unacceptably wide joints between the stones or impossibly intricate block trimming to contend with.

right: *The simple grey zig-zag perfectly complements the straight border, an easy but effective design touch. Notice the cut ends at the straight edge of the path. Hire a block splitter to cut these angled infill pieces neatly.*

A GRAVEL WALKWAY WITH BRICK PATTERNS

You can mix gravel with smooth slabs or block pavers to create attractive patterns and contrasts. The blocks also help to keep gravel off lawns and beds. This simple path is cheap and easy to make. Rake the ground to remove any debris, level it and tread it down. Cover the compacted earth with a good layer of moistened sand and flatten it.

1 Lay a line of bricks from side to side, level with the straight edges – here, pavers set on edge. Make these firm and level. Fill the triangular spaces with shingle and tread it down gently. Do not to push the bricks out of line before it has settled.

2 Edge this simple but effective formal path with suitable plants. The path is cheap and easy to make and you only need to cut a few bricks as they do not dominate the design. Gravel is an ideal alternative to grass for narrow paths such as this.

Paving for areas of heavy use

WHAT YOU WILL NEED

Skill level:

DIY experience required

Best time to do:

Any dry, non-frosty

period. Summer is ideal

Special tools required:

Club hammer; spirit

level; brick-laying

trowel; shovel; cement

mixer for large areas

Time required:

Two weekends/four

days

WHAT YOU WILL NEED

• Ready-mixed concrete
• Polythene sheeting or damp sacking
• Wooden shuttering
• Hardboard expansion joints
• Mortar (masonry cement and chemical plasticiser)
• Water
• Club hammer, spirit level and wooden straightedge
• Wooden spacers
• Shovel and brick-laying trowel

If a patio surface is intended to support a considerable weight it will be necessary to prepare a concrete base on which to lay the paving slabs. Excavate the site to a depth of at least 150mm(6in) – more if the subsoil is unstable – and lay a concrete base a minimum of 100mm(4in) thick. You can use ready-mixed concrete or mix your own with one part of cement to five parts of combined sand and 20mm(¾in) aggregate. Set up wooden shuttering around the area to give the base a neat square edge, tamp the concrete down well, level the surface with a long straightedge laid across the formwork and remove any excess material. Give the base a slight fall across its width, and incorporate full-width vertical expansion joints of hardboard or similar material every 3m(10ft) to prevent cracking. Cover concrete with plastic to protect from rain or frost, or damp sacking if it is hot and sunny. Leave for at least three days.

2 Lower each slab gently onto its mortar bed and tamp it down evenly with the handle of a club hammer to compress the mortar.

Use a fairly sloppy mortar mix (1 part cement, 1 part lime, or a measure of plasticiser and 6 parts building sand), so that it is easy to spread beneath the slabs.

Use a concrete mix of 1 part cement, 2½ parts concreting sand and 3½ parts 20mm(¾ in) aggregate or a mix of 1 part cement to 5 parts of combined aggregates.

1 To give the slabs adequate support, place the mortar on the concrete base in a square beneath the edges of the slab and add more mortar beneath the centre of the slab.

3 After placing the slab, bedding it down and setting it to the correct fall, insert small wooden spacers between it and its neighbours to ensure an even pointing gap.

right: *Slabs laid onto concrete could be quite barren. But the picture shows that given a helping hand, creeping herbs, alpines and cottage favourites like viola will colonise and soften expanses of paving.*

A POINTING GUIDE

If the pointing mortar stains the slab surface as you work, reduce the problem by using a guide made from a plywood offcut. Cut a slot into the plywood to match the joint width and lay the offcut on the slabs. Fill the joints through the slot.

Use a spirit level and a long straightedge to check level and fall.

4 Continue laying the slabs in this way, checking that the surface has the correct fall. Tamp down out-of-line slabs a little more if necessary.

5 When all the slabs are laid and levelled, remove the wooden spacers and point the joints with a fairly dry mortar mix. Force it well into the joints with the edge of a pointing trowel. Alternatively, brush dry mortar into the cracks between the slabs and water it with a fine rose.

Laying random stone

Random stone or 'crazy' paving, is made from randomly shaped stone pieces or broken concrete paving slabs that fit together like pieces of a jigsaw. The gaps between are pointed with mortar which bonds the stones to a stable base layer. Random paving can look very attractive if you fit the pieces together carefully and neatly detail the pointing. An old concrete surface would make an ideal foundation for a driveway or parking place; well-rammed coarse aggregate is suitable for light-duty areas such as a patio or garden path. Start laying the stones at the perimeter, using pieces with one straight side and use a long wooden straightedge as you lay down more stones to ensure that they are level. If necessary, check that the stones are laid to a slight fall to allow surface water to drain off. Only spread as much mortar as you can cover with paving pieces within the time it takes for the mortar to set.

WHAT YOU WILL NEED

• Random assortment of stone or broken paving
• Mortar (see previous pages for recipe and tools needed)
• Brick-laying trowel, wooden straightedge, spirit level and club hammer

1 To break up a stone or improve the fit, lodge it between two stones and crack it cleanly with a firm hammer blow.

2 Sort stones into groups: corner stones with two adjacent square edges, perimeter stones with one straight edge, and large, irregularly shaped stones.

3 A solid foundation is essential for crazy paving. Spread a bed of fairly sloppy mortar along the perimeter of the base layer. See previous pages for the correct 'recipe' for the mortar.

4 Choose relatively large stones with two adjacent straight edges to form the corners of square or rectangular paved areas. Set the corner stone in place, tamp it down into the mortar bed as shown.

5 Place the next perimeter stone on the mortar bed in line with the first, tamp down and check levels.

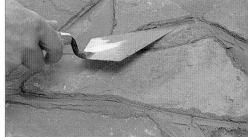

6 Complete one edge of the area, including the next corner stone. Then start building up the jigsaw effect with large and smaller stones.

7 As you extend the paving, use a spirit level and a long straight-edge to check that the stones are level (or have a constant fall).

8 Allow the mortar bed to harden overnight before filling and pointing the joints. Draw the trowel point along the joint to leave a ridge and two sloping bevels.

Allow a slope of 1 in 40 away from adjacent buildings or across free-standing paths and drives.

TERRACOTTA TILES AND EDGING

Secure terracotta edging strips in place with a strip of mortar along each side. Slope it as shown and check that it is low enough to allow the paving slab to butt up against it. Terracotta rope edging is sold in lengths of about 610mm(2ft). Use a strong mortar – 1 part cement to 3 or 4 parts sand, plus added plasticiser – to bed the edging in place.

1 Set the rope edging and corner posts in place. Spread a bed of sloppy mortar over the area to be paved. Place the corner tile first, then add further tiles. To cut a tile, reverse and place on a sand bed. Score a line with a bolster chisel and straightedge and cut along it with a hammer and chisel.

2 With a few tiles in place, check that they are level when viewed against the edging. Use a spirit level to ensure that each row is level across the tiled area. Try not to get any of the mortar mix onto the surface of the tile as it will show up against the terracotta colouring and spoil the effect.

3 Decorative tiles form a border to plain terracotta pavers, each equivalent in size to four tiles. Place the paver on the mortar bed, tamp it down and check the levels. This module shows how the edging, tiles and pavers are coordinated in size. The edging length matches three tile widths.

A flight of steps

Skill level:

Some experience of

bricklaying useful

Best time to do:

Any dry, non-frosty

period

Special tools required:

Bricklaying trowel;

spirit level; club

hammer; brick bolster

Time required:

Most of a weekend

WHAT YOU WILL NEED

• Frost proof bricks
• Textured paving slabs for treads
• Mortar
• Wooden straightedge, spirit level, club hammer, brick bolster, bricklayer's trowel

If your garden slopes steeply and is terraced, you will need to construct steps for access from one level to the next. These are more than simply functional; a well-designed flight of steps can be an important visual element in the overall landscaping plan. Construct them from materials that complement those used elsewhere in the garden for walls and paved surfaces. Bricks have a neat, formal look; decorative stone walling blocks give a softer appearance. Paving slabs are ideal for forming the treads. Where you are linking two terraced areas, you can design the steps in a number of ways. The flight can descend at right angles to the wall or be built parallel with it – often a better solution where one level is higher than the other or where space is restricted on the lower level. A rectangular flight is the simplest to build, but you could create a series of semicircular steps instead.

CUTTING BRICKS

If you need to cut a brick to size, start by marking the cutting line on the brick and score it all round with the tip of a brick bolster (bricklayer's chisel). Place the brick on a bed of sand and drive the chisel with blows from a club hammer to break the brick at the marked cutting position. The sand helps to spread the impact along the cutting line.

VARIATIONS ON THE THEME

Of course you can also make steps entirely out of brick pavers, but there is a lot of work involved in this and it is much easier to use larger decorative stone walling blocks. These have a face like natural stone, with flat tops and bottoms so that they can be laid and bonded easily. They are also easier to cut, if necessary, using ordinary masonry tools.

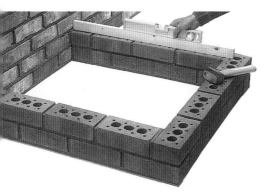

1 The first step comprises two courses of bricks on a foundation. Start the second course with a half-brick to maintain the stretcher bond.

2 Build up internal supporting walls to carry the rest of the structure. You can use old bricks for this, and leave the joints unpointed.

3 Using a spirit level at every stage, build up the brickwork for the second tread on top of the walls. Add two more courses internally.

4 Place the treads on the first step. Trowel on a generous mortar bed, lower the slabs into place and tamp them down so that they have a slight fall towards the front edge to help drainage and prevent puddles that could freeze.

5 Repeat the process for the second step. Then fill and point the joints between the pairs of slabs, and also the gaps at the rear of each tread. This two-step flight will use the face of the terrace wall as the final riser.

6 Complete the flight by bedding two slabs in place at the top of the flight, with their edges just projecting beyond the face of the terrace wall.

For a good grip in wet or wintry weather, choose slabs with a textured surface for steps.

Decorative Surfaces

There are so many different ways to surface the garden, and some of the best effects are achieved through the clever mixing and matching of materials, including plants. The differences between adjacent areas can also be given a contrasting feel by simply changing the flooring effects. Our view of lawns tends to be restricted to grass turf, but you can use several kinds of plants for soft surfacing the garden. The shape of a lawn also has a tremendous influence on the design of the garden and even a few simple changes can make a dramatic improvement. Throughout this section we will consider several exciting and stylish options for giving the garden a makeover, including decking, the use of cobbles, mosaic floors, contemporary gravel gardens and how to make your lawn a design feature in its own right.

Making a feature of your lawn

GRASS SCULPTING

In a large lawn you can experiment by allowing different areas to be mown with the blades set to different heights. This technique will create curving abstract ground patterns that you can change periodically.

Lawns form clear, flat open areas that create a feeling of spaciousness. The colour and texture of a lawn makes a pleasing contrast with other kinds of garden surfacing such as gravel, paving and decking. And in winter, when the garden has largely died down, the emerald green of a lawn is a cheering sight. Lawns act as a green foil for the plants and features contained in the garden but can also become features in their own right.

Sometimes all you need to do to transform the whole look of a garden is to change the shape and layout of the lawned areas. For example, if you have the traditional long rectangular lawn with

above: *This circular lawn is edged in brick, which not only emphasises the shape of the lawn but effectively separates it from the contrasting gravel area. Features such as the curving stone bench complement and reinforce the circular theme. Notice how the eye travels round to the perimeter to the bird bath, through the planting to the hidden pathway beyond.*

straight-edged flower borders, you could superimpose two or three interlocking or 'kissing' circles over the rectangle and cut the new lawn edge making the borders curved. The circles could be defined more clearly by edging them with brick set just below the cutting height of your mower. A circular or semi-circular lawn that replaces a square one can also make a small garden feel much larger because the eye follows the perimeter of the lawn in an uninterrupted ark. The circular lawn is also a useful solution for irregularly or awkwardly shaped gardens such as triangles. Once the borders are planted up and the boundaries disappear, the pleasing shape of the lawn becomes a central focus.

Do:

• Consider changing the shape of your lawn to improve the garden's design
• Keep the design simple with straight lines or broad curves
• Emphasise the shape with a decorative lawn edging of brick or stone
• Use circular lawns as a solution to awkwardly shaped sites
• Contrast areas of lawn with other surface textures for year-round interest

Don't:

• Create difficulties with mowing or maintenance of lawns by growing in shady or inaccessible areas
• Allow gravel to be walked onto the lawn. Small stones can ruin mower blades
• Forget to maintain a clean cut edge in more formal gardens or where the lawn shape is geometric

right: Lawns can help to lead the eye through the garden. Here a series of stepping stones adds further emphasis as the green continues beneath the rose arch to a hidden area beyond. The look of stepping stones in grass is far softer and more relaxed than gravel or paving, and the stones also prevent the grass being damaged by footfall in wet weather.

Lawns can be used to subtly guide a person through the garden along the route you wish them to take. It is hard to resist following a long, sinuous ribbon of green as it winds through the planting revealing previously hidden aspects of the garden. If you have a long narrow garden, a serpentine lawn such as this can create exciting design possibilities. Remember, circles and broad, gentle curves feel restful. Wiggly lawn edges are too 'busy' visually to be relaxing and are harder to mow. If you have this kind of lawn margin, consider smoothing out the lines a little.

If you want to introduce an informal feel, consider converting part of a large lawned area into wildflower meadow and plant bulbs in naturalistic drifts. The contrast between mown and long grass is very pleasing and you can vary the path route with ease.

Laying and shaping a lawn

Skill level:

Beginner gardener

Best time to do:

Mid- to late spring or

autumn or during mild

spells in winter

Special tools required:

Digging fork

Time required:

May take a weekend –

a day to prepare

ground and a day

to lay the lawn

WHAT YOU WILL NEED

- Rolls of fresh, good quality turf
- A plank or board to work from
- Digging fork
- Potting mix or sifted soil to fill gaps
- Grass seed (to match mixture used in the turf)
- Soft broom
- Hose pipe with soft spray attachment

The quickest way to get a 'usable' lawn is unquestionably by laying turf. In essence, you are transplanting grass to your garden. However, and this is where any difficulties might arise, you have to remember that you are dealing with living plants. This means that, from the moment the turf is laid, you must on no account allow it to become dry. If it does, the individual turves will shrink, gaps will appear between them and they will dry out even quicker. Shrinking involves movement and movement will prevent new roots forming and growing into the underlying ground.

Soil preparation is just the same – and just as important – as for sowing seed and, like seed mixtures, there are different grades of turf available for the quality of lawn you require. This will be reflected in the price of the turf. Cheap turf may be broken, uneven, thin, or even full of weeds. Beware! Lay turf at any time but autumn and spring are best since the weather is usually mild and the soil damp. Winter is acceptable, but do not lay turves during prolonged cold spells. When laying or reshaping a lawn with an irregular outline, use a hosepipe or long piece of heavy rope to mark out the perimeter and then replace with pegs and string. Do not try to cut the edge straight after laying new turf. Wait for it to knit together.

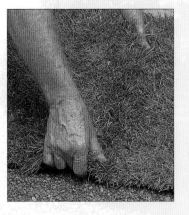

1 Lay onto a very well firmed and trodden base, levelled with a rake. To avoid gaps, leave a hump at the end of each turf as you place it against the previous one, to be pushed flat later. Stagger the ends of adjoining turves, as this makes a stronger bond.

2 This is the first row of turf, so the plank from which you should work is on bare ground. When laying subsequent rows, the plank should be positioned on the last row you laid, to distribute your weight across the newly laid turf and help it bed down.

3 After laying each turf, push down the hump you left at the end to make a tight fit against the neighbouring turf. This will go a long way to preventing gaps due to shrinking if the turf should dry out. In any event, you should keep the turves well watered.

EDGING A LAWN

A well-kept lawn makes the perfect backdrop to the whole garden and small details, such as well-made lawn edges, make all the difference to the overall effect.

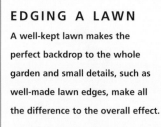

To keep the lawn edge looking tidy, use a half-moon edger to slice away a vertical strip about 7.5cm(3in) deep all round the perimeter of the lawn. Repeat regularly.

VARIATIONS ON THE THEME

To mark out a circular lawn, fill a bottle with sand. Attach one end of a piece of string (length equalling radius), and tie the other end to a marker at the centre of the lawn. Keeping the string taught, pour the sand as you walk around. Use a half-moon edger to cut along the line and create the circle.

4 To make sure that the turf is hard against its neighbour lengthways, tap it into place with a fork. No great force is needed; use just enough to get rid of the gap. Press or pat down each turf, so that it makes good contact with the ground. This removes any air pockets.

5 This is how the pattern of turf should look once you have laid down a number of turves. As you complete each row of turves or when the whole lawn is finished, fill in any gaps between the turves with a sprinkling of soil to prevent the edges drying out.

6 When you have sprinkled the potting mix or sifted soil along all the joins, use a soft broom to brush over the whole lawn, both to work the dressing down into any cracks and to tidy up the area. If you find wider gaps in the lawn, sprinkle seed on top of them.

7 Just as when sowing a new lawn, water the newly turfed area thoroughly when you have finished. This not only washes any remaining soil into the cracks, but also ensures that the turves have adequate moisture. They must remain moist as they get established.

Placing stepping stones in a lawn

Skill level:

Beginner gardener

Best time to do:

Any fine spell when the

ground is not too wet

Special tools required:

Sharp border spade

Time required:

Half a day, for a

relatively short run of

stepping stones

WHAT YOU WILL NEED

• Sharp border spade
• Fine gravel or sand to make up levels
• Small paving slabs or random pieces of flat stone such as slate
• Quantity of fine dry soil
• Small amount of grass seed to cover gaps
• Soft broom

Comparatively speaking, small lawns get much heavier wear than large ones. In a tiny garden you have no choice but to use the same route across the lawn to the washing line or shed. And there is probably only one convenient, sunny spot to put garden seats on a nice day when you want to sit outside. So you use the same patch of grass all the time. No wonder it soon starts to look patchy and worn out. In winter, worn areas of grass become slippery with liverwort or algae, or just turn to mud which gets trodden indoors. In summer, heavily used grass cannot grow fast enough to replace itself, and thin patches let in moss and weeds which makes the lawn look scruffy and ill-kempt. And if you keep walking over the same route, you eventually wear a track across the lawn where the water collects after rain and the grass never grows. The best way to keep a small lawn looking perfect all the time is to stay off it. For a real enthusiast with a fine lawn and no family, this is a feasible option. For the rest of us, stepping stones make an excellent compromise!

1 Instead of wearing a track through a small lawn, sink a few 'stepping stones' into the lawn to walk on. Rest the slabs on the grass; cut round them with the back of a spade.

2 Remove the slab and lift the turf. (If you can leave the slab standing for several days, the grass under it turns yellow and leaves a shape for cutting round.) Remove all the turf, leaving clean vertical cuts.

3 Offer up the slab. If it is proud of the surrounding turf, make the hole deeper. If too deep, add a layer of gravel. The mower needs to pass straight over the slab, so it must be slightly recessed in the lawn.

VARIATIONS ON THE THEME

Stepping stones are not always purely functional. They can help to create a carefree atmosphere and look well in semi-wild areas. Most importantly, they lead the eye very effectively. Use them to draw attention to a sheltered sitting place, a pool or an ornamental feature, such as a decorative birdhouse. Or allow them to guide you towards some secret corner of the garden.

4 Press the slab down well so that it sits securely. The snug fit and vertical sides of the hole help to hold it in place.

5 Fill narrow gaps with fine dry soil or potting mix tipped onto the slab and brushed into the cracks. For wider gaps, mix in grass seed.

6 Set an irregular row of slabs into the lawn, a comfortable walking pace apart. The path will be firm and dry underfoot and the lawn remains in good condition.

above: *Randomly shaped pieces of stone make an attractive feature. Here they lead to a shallow flight of steps through a narrow gap in the planting.*

left: *A more contemporary look is achieved using rectangular paving slabs laid close together to form a broad pathway. Because grass grows between the stones, the lawn effectively continues uninterrupted. This approach is useful for areas of heavy traffic.*

Lawn edging

WHAT YOU WILL NEED

• Bricks or paving slabs
• Sand or ready-mix dryish mortar for bedding the edging units onto
• Sharp border spade for cutting the lawn edge and removing turf
• Wooden straight edge and spirit level
• Club hammer to tamp down and level edge units
• Sand or dry mortar mix and a broom to brush it into the joints

Mowing and edging are two of the most time consuming jobs in the garden, but the latter can be almost completely eliminated by the installation of a mowing strip. This consists of an edging of brick or flat stones set just below the lawn so that the mower can run freely over the surface. Brick pavers, which are normally laid on concrete foundations, are ideal for edging circular or curving lawns. The curve is easily accommodated by leaving wedge-shaped mortar gaps between the blocks. Even wider mowing strips made from stone or concrete paving are useful in less formal situations where summer herbaceous plants and shrubs are planted to spill out over the lawn. Under normal circumstances this would kill the grass beneath and cause problems with mowing access.

A formal brick or paved mowing strip defines the lawn beautifully and looks well in a contemporary urban setting where the lines are crisp and neat. You can use mowing strips to create patterns within the lawned areas. For example, where a rectangular lawn has been re-shaped to look like three interlocking circles, instead of confining the mowing strip to the perimeter, continue it round each of the circles to create a design. You can do the same thing with gravel areas and instead of circles you could use interlocking rectangles.

MAINTAINING AN EDGE

To neaten up the edge of the mowing strip and to prevent lawn grass from encroaching too far, periodically run over it with a nylon-line trimmer. Alternatively, use a half-moon cutter or sharp border spade to re-cut the edge next to the blocks or rectangular paving pieces.

left: *A wide paving strip allows plants to tumble over the edge of the border in a natural way without affecting the lawn or getting caught up with mowing.*

right: *A mowing strip not only serves a useful purpose at the edge of the lawn — it can also look striking and be something of a decorative feature in its own right.*

Alternatives to grass

above: *Lawn chamomile (Chamaemelum nobile 'Treneague'), can replace a small lawn where foot traffic is very light. It has a fruity aroma.*

Variations in height and texture are an all-important part of good garden design. Unrelieved lawns covering a large area can be rather boring, but if you create new island beds or flower borders, will you have time to maintain them? This question is particularly important in front gardens, which tend to be more public and therefore less pleasurable to work in. In a small garden, it may be impractical to have a lawn, especially where access for the mower is difficult, but you may still want a relatively low expanse of greenery to contrast with paving and surrounding plantings. Low-growing, spreading evergreens such as certain hebes, *Euonymus fortunei* varieties, and *Vinca minor* varieties can also be used as an alternative ground cover to lawns.

For larger areas, the many types of prostrate or spreading conifers – for example, junipers – can be used to spread and cover the ground quite quickly, creating a pleasing evergreen tapestry of greens, blues, greys and gold. Heathers are traditional partners, and interesting effects can be achieved by filling gaps in a mixed conifer/heather planting with a cobble mulch and the occasional larger boulder, or by placing taller, jagged rock specimens in small groups to give height amongst surrounding plants.

Do:

• Replace very small areas of lawn with low-maintenance ground-cover planting, especially if mower access is difficult
• Create textural interest in a large lawned or paved area by planting with evergreen shrubs, conifers and ground-cover plants
• Consider planting through a weed-suppressant membrane
• Experiment with decorative mulches

Don't:

• Use grass under trees or in the shade of buildings
• Use vigorous ground-cover plants that could spread into the existing lawn
• Use too many different kinds of plant in the same small area. Stick to one kind if you mean to provide an area that mimics grass

above: *Ground cover plants can look especially effective when planted in borders that run up beneath trees. They bring a touch of the forest to the garden, particularly when they are combined with bulbs.*

left: *Conifers and heathers are traditional partners and can make excellent low-maintenance ground cover, providing interest in colour and texture all year round.*

Such borders would be easy to maintain once the plants had matured and covered the ground but to be sure that you are really keeping your work to a minimum, you could also plant through a weed-proof membrane.

To create contrast in large areas of paving, creeping evergreen herbs such as thymes and non-flowering chamomile, can be grown singly to create the effect of a lawn without the need for mowing. Many of these plants thrive on relatively poor dry soil where grass would suffer. Grass also has a tough time under trees, where the ground is not only shaded but often very dry and full of roots. Lawns also suffer in the shade cast by buildings and north-facing fences where moss can take over. For shade ground-cover, especially under trees, choose any of the plain green or white-variegated ivies.

Planting green carpets

Skill level:

Beginner gardener

Best time to do:

Late spring and early

summer

Special tools required:

After ground

preparation, just a

planting trowel

Time required:

A couple of hours,

once ground has

been prepared

WHAT YOU WILL NEED

• For sun and sharp drainage, creeping plants, e.g. *Thymus* 'Doone Valley', *Chamaemelum nobile* 'Treneague'. For shade, *Soleirolia soleirolii, Mentha requienii*
• Rounded cobbles and boulders
• A trowel
• Grit or gravel to lighten heavy soil for sun-lovers
• Organic matter to retain moisture for the shade plantings

Grass is the surface most people automatically choose to cover those parts of the garden where they do not intend to grow flowers and shrubs. It acts rather like a self-regenerating carpet, and makes a natural green backdrop that sets off trees and flowers perfectly. However, to keep grass looking good it needs regular mowing and if it gets heavy wear – for instance from children and dogs playing on it – then feeding and occasional repairs will also be needed. Grass is not always the easy option it is often believed to be. You can make lawn care easier by using paving or gravel in places that get heavy wear, such as the sitting-out area, and by laying hard paths along routes where

SOLEIROLIA AMONGST PEBBLES

Grass will not grow in a very shady area, but helxine or ivy will thrive. Combine a cobblestone surface with these low creeping plants to make an attractive feature. Use this idea between paving stones, as an edging to a path or as unusual ground cover in a problem area.

1 Prepare the soil well, adding plenty of organic matter. Put in the plants 23-30cm(9-12in) apart. Helxine can become invasive close to lawns.

2 Select smooth, evenly-sized, coloured cobblestones. Press them into place between the plants. Group them in clusters if you do not want a solid surface.

3 Tuck more cobbles around the plants and bed them down firmly. Move any that create large areas of one colour; aim for a speckled mix.

4 Water the whole area to get the plants off to a good start and to firm the stones into place. This is particularly important if you are going to walk on them. The end result is a very self-sufficient feature. The cobbles act like a mulch, preventing weed seeds from germinating.

Above: A thyme lawn makes a very pretty feature in a decorative 'edible garden'. Plant a mixture of creeping varieties in a random pattern. Well-drained soil and a sunny spot are essential. Dig in plenty of gravel for good drainage.

you frequently walk, say from the back door to the shed or washing line. But in some situations, other forms of soft surface may be more suitable than grass. For instance, under trees, where grass does not thrive due to heavy shade or dry soil, a surface of bark chippings looks pleasing and natural but needs no work to maintain. On a slope that is difficult to mow, ground cover plants grown close together make a dense layer that smothers out weeds, looks good all year round and flowers seasonally. In a hot, dry, sunny spot where grass needs frequent watering, a thyme lawn made of spreading varieties grown through gravel creates a low leafy effect, yet needs no mowing or irrigation; it is also delightfully scented.

THYME PATH

Thyme is a most useful garden plant. Its tiny leaves and dense habit create a carpet, cushion or low hedge according to variety, and are ideal for softening harder landscaped features, such as walls, paths and edges of containers. Creeping thyme roots where the stems touch the soil, so plants are very resilient.

1 To plant a creeping thyme beside a path, first dig a planting pocket in the soil the right size for the pot.

2 Press in the plant, leaving no gaps around the rootball. All the foliage should remain on the surface and not be half-buried.

3 A creeping variety of thyme is perfect for growing between patio slabs or alongside a path. It spreads and softens the edges of the stones and survives being trodden on occasionally. The pungent scent of fresh thyme perfumes the air each time you do so.

Making a conifer and heather bed

Skill level:

Beginner gardener

(seek garden centre

advice if necessary)

Best time to do:

Any moist mild spell.

Early autumn is the

ideal time

Special tools required:

None: general garden

tools only

Time required:

Up to a whole weekend

WHAT YOU WILL NEED

• A soil test kit to check your soil pH
• A varied selection of plants that combine well and will provide colour and interest year-round
• Organic matter to improve the quality of the soil
• Tools to dig over and prepare the bed and a trowel for planting heathers and young conifers
• Decorative mulch of bark or cocoa shells

Heathers and conifers naturally associate well together and need the same conditions - an open, sunny site with plenty of fresh air, and neutral or acid soil that neither dries out nor becomes waterlogged. But if you have alkaline soil, the winter and spring flowering heathers from the *Erica carnea, E. × darleyensis* or *E. erigena* groups will thrive provided you dig in plenty of organic matter. You can grow heathers and conifers in traditional beds and borders, but one way to plant them is in island beds – informal shapes such as 'teardrops' cut out of the lawn. Being open on all sides, such beds are easy to weed, and because more light and air can reach the plants, they tend to be healthier and relatively pest-free. The secret of an attractive heather and conifer bed lies in teaming plants with highly contrasting shapes, colours and textures. Upright, flame- and dome-shaped conifers contrast with bushy or open branching shapes, and all are set off by a continuous carpet of heather underneath. On neutral to acid soil you can choose heathers from all the main groups to give colour virtually all year round. Forms of *Calluna vulgaris* which need neutral to acid soil, flower from summer through autumn and many are noted for having vividly coloured new growth in spring, yellow- or orange- tinted summer foliage and for developing rich hues as the weather starts to turn colder. They flower mainly in late summer and autumn.

1 Space the conifers, allowing for the size they will reach in ten years; see the plant label. Surround them with heathers spaced 30-45cm(12-18in) apart; these plants should make a complete carpet within two years.

2 Water all the plants very thoroughly. If the pots are dry when you buy them, soak the roots for a few hours before planting so that the rootball gets wet right through. The best way is to submerge the pots in water.

3 Finish with decorative mulch to help retain moisture. Cocoa shells or bark look very good with this type of planting. Both are slightly acidic, and the chocolate smell deters cats from using your newly planted bed as an earth closet.

BUYING TIPS

Heathers are sold as one- or two-year-old plants and occasionally as larger specimens. They grow quickly, so if you don't mind waiting a couple of years for them to fill out it is worth buying the cheaper one-year-olds. Heathers are best planted in groups of the same variety, so buy three, five or seven plants depending on the size of the area that you wish to cover. Bargains are also to be found with young conifer plants, especially carpeting and spreading varieties of junipers, of which there are many colourful and interesting forms. Always buy healthy, well-looking specimens.

above: *This beautifully balanced conifer and heather bed is probably around ten years old and contains plants that are often described as 'dwarf'. Do your research thoroughly before buying your heathers and conifers to ensure the right mix and positioning of the plants.*

left: *Heathers make superb ground cover, forming close mats or undulating hummocks of evergreen foliage and flowers from late summer through to late spring, depending on the variety.*

Versatile and decorative gravel

Gravel has a myriad uses from practical to decorative. Dig it in to improve the drainage of heavy soils and to give sun-loving herbs and alpines the conditions in which to thrive. Use it as a cheap surfacing material for paths, patios and driveways or as a decorative, weed-resistant infill for awkward spaces. Gravel blends easily with plantings to give a soft, relaxed feel and creates an interesting 'dry' garden or Mediterranean effect when used as a weed-suppressant mulch for borders. When planting a gravel feature such as the circular garden illustrated on the opposite page, lay down

below left: The theme of this unusual and highly attractive area is contrasting form and texture. Hostas, grasses and thymes provide an array of foliage shapes and mini-sleepers set into the ground anchor the whole display.

a sheet of permeable membrane before starting to radically reduce the amount of weeding required. Gravel also has quite a contemporary look when combined with certain plants and materials and is excellent for surfacing tiny town gardens where a lawn would be impractical. It can also create an Oriental feel when combined with stone, pebbles and plants with a Japanese feel.

Gravel comes ready-bagged from garden centres or builder's merchants in different grades and colours depending on the effect you want and it can also be purchased loose by the tonne or cubic metre from builder's merchants or a local gravel pit. The latter is more economical and useful for creating large areas such as driveways or a Zen garden. Match the size or grade of gravel to the area you wish to cover or to the size and texture of foliage you are combining it

Do:

• Combine gravel with a weed-suppressant membrane
• Combine gravel with grasses, 'silverlings' and architectural plants for a Mediterranean effect
• Use gravel as an inexpensive surfacing or temporary stop-gap until you can afford paving
• Use gravel to fill awkward spaces and to provide textural contrast

Don't:

• Use fine gravel in the garden if you have a problem with cats. Use gravel of approximately 3–4cm or 1½ in diameter which is too heavy for them to scratch up
• Use fine gravel for areas to be walked on. It sticks in shoe treads and can be brought into the house
• Allow gravel to stray into lawn grass. Use a deep mowing edge as a separation
• Plant nuisance self-seeders next to a gravel area

below: *A circle of gravel, mirroring the round patio beyond, replaces what would conventionally be a lawn area. The warm golden gravel tones beautifully with the surrounding pebble path and stonework and makes a lovely foil for the planting.*

with. Gravel also looks well when contrasted with different sized pebbles and cobbles to give an interestingly textured surface.

Gravel is a wonderfully easy material to manage once it has been laid, requiring only occasional raking and topping-up to look consistently good. If you do not use a permeable membrane beneath it, it may also need weeding, but so long as the area is not too big it is easy to pull out the odd weed before it becomes too big. Avoid nuisance self-seeders.

Planting a mediterranean gravel garden

Skill level:

Beginner gardener

Best time to do:

Anytime the ground is

workable. For more

tender plants, late

spring is best

Special tools required:

None

Time required:

Once the ground is

prepared, about a day

Mulching is a useful technique used to avoid routine weeding. It works by starving germinating weed seedlings of light. Mulching also reduces moisture loss and insulates roots from extremes of heat and cold. Gravel can be used to form an area of sharp drainage around alpines, silver-leaved plants and other subjects like herbs that can be sensitive to winter wet and is one of the most attractive mulching materials. To be effective, spread it to 5cm (2in) deep. It will not prevent strong perennial weeds growing through, so these will have to be spot treated with systemic weedkiller or dug out beforehand. An even more effective alternative is to lay a membrane beneath.

right: *Even if you have laid a membrane beneath a gravel mulch, it is still possible to create the impression of plants that have casually set seed and flourished between the cobbles and paving stones. Here honey-scented white alyssum and a small-leaved ivy have been planted along the edge of the slabs in a naturalistic way that softens the area and helps to create a relaxed impression.*

WHAT YOU WILL NEED

• Assorted plants including – tussock forming grasses; creeping and cushion-forming alpines and herbs; silver-leaved and daisy-flowered perennials and shrubs with a Mediterranean look
• Mulch membrane
• Wire 'pegs'
• Gravel
• Scissors or blade
• Trowel
• Pre-prepared bed free of weeds

1 Cover the soil with perforated black plastic or landscape fabric. Secure it with pegs sold for the purpose or bent wire prongs. Spread a 5cm(2in)-thick layer of pea gravel with rounded edges.

2 Decide where you wish to put in a plant and scrape back the gravel to reveal the plastic. Make two cuts crossing each other in the middle of the planting site, each one twice the diameter of the pot.

3 Peel back the corners of the plastic to expose the soil beneath; place stones or gravel on the flaps to hold them back while you put in the plant. Scoop out soil from the planting hole with trowel.

7 When the plant is out of its pot, make sure that the planting hole is large enough to take the rootball. Sit it in position, with its best side to the front.

8 Fill in the space around the rootball with soil and firm down lightly. Water well and then push back the plastic flaps, so that they fit snugly around the plant. Holding the plant over to one side, sweep the spare gravel back round the plant with your hand, so that all the plastic is completely hidden.

right: *This scheme would look equally at home in a cottage garden or a car parking area covered with gravel. In the latter case, roughly surround the plants with large stones as an early warning!*

PLANTING BULBS UNDER GRAVEL

Bulbs such as *Iris reticulata* (shown below) can be naturalised to add spring interest to any well-drained area that is fairly dry in summer, such as gravelled areas in a patio. Use them to create small 'cameo' features next to a garden seat, ornament or statue.

1 Scoop out a depression and scatter the bulbs at random. Press in and twist to ensure contact with the soil.

2 When the soil is level with the surrounding area, add a thin layer of stone chippings as a mulch and decorative finish.

3 Dwarf irises (*Iris reticulata*) flower in blue or purple with yellow or orange markings in early spring. Up to 15cm(6in) tall.

Osteospermum 'Stardust'

Armeria formosa

Lavandula angustifolia 'Munstead'

Stachys byzantina

Helianthemum 'Sunbeam'

Nepeta × faassenii

Livening up your patio

Skill level:

Paving experience is

useful

Best time to do:

Late spring is ideal,

when plenty of good

alpine plants are

available

Special tools required:

Crowbar or hired

power hammer

Time required:

A whole weekend

One way of livening up a large area of paving is to make sunken beds by removing occasional slabs and planting in the spaces, or to plant low-growing plants into the cracks between slabs. You could even combine the two ideas for a bigger, more imaginative planting scheme. Decide where you want to create a bed and stand the plants, still in their pots, on the slab you have decided to remove so that you can judge the effect. If you are laying a new patio, it is simple to plan for such beds in advance. Instead of laying the usual rubble and concrete base over the whole area, leave the soil clear where your bed is to go. Improve the existing garden soil (assuming it is reasonably good) with organic matter, such as well-rotted garden compost, and pave round it. If you want to take up slabs from an existing paved area, chip away the cement from between the slabs and lever them out with a crowbar. If they are completely bedded into cement, you may not be able to avoid cracking them, and you may need a power hammer to remove them, together with the foundations beneath them, until you reach bare soil. Remove as much rubble as possible.

WHAT YOU WILL NEED

• Selection of drought-tolerant carpeting and hummock forming plants – low-growing and dwarf shrubs and conifers; herbs; alpines, grasses
• Gravel mulch and perhaps pebbles and cobbles
• Trowel, crowbar or hired power hammer
• Well-rotted compost, plus some slow-release fertiliser to mix into very poor ground

1 Lever out the slab – this one is easy as it is loose-laid over soil. Excavate the hole so that there is room to put in plenty of good soil and slow release fertiliser.

2 If the existing soil is fairly good, simply add suitable organic matter to improve the texture and help moisture retention. Add grit for alpines.

3 Put the largest plant in the centre of the new bed. This compact, bushy potentilla will flower all summer. It spreads quickly and could fill the space.

VARIATIONS ON THE THEME You could also use small pebbles, cobbles and rounded boulders to contrast with gravel and paving. And within this varied surface, why not create a bubbling fountain made by installing an underground reservoir with a small submersible pump? Cover the tank with a rigid sheet of wire mesh and camouflage with more cobbles.

SOWING SEEDS

Sprinkle seeds of alpine flowers, alyssum or creeping thymes thinly in the cracks between paving slabs – useful where gaps are too narrow for planting. Sprinkle a little fine grit over the top, barely burying the seeds, then water well. Keep the area watered until the seedlings grow into small plants. Thin them out – do not transplant them; once they reach a fair size, undisturbed rock plant seedlings are more drought-tolerant than transplants.

above: *Tip the tiny seeds into your hand and sprinkle the barest pinch of seed very thinly into the crack in the paving.*

4 Planting compact rock plants in the corners 'ties in' the bed with rock plants growing in cracks between other paving slabs nearby. Allow room for growth.

5 Choose plants that will spill out over the paving and make the selection different in colour and shape to avoid things looking too symmetrical. Mulch with gravel.

right: *This semi-paved area is a visual treat and shows the potential for transforming a boring area of solid paving. Carpeting succulents such as sedums and sempervivums are reminiscent of hot sunny climes and are perfect for a sun-drenched patio. The spiky black-leaved* Ophiopogon planiscapus *'Nigrescens' makes a dramatic contrast.*

Pebble, tile and brick surfaces

above: *Detail is everything! Here cobbles laid on end form a low edging to an area of granite sets.*

In a small garden where space is at a premium, the fine detail of paving and edging takes on even greater significance. And you can have great fun making all kinds of patterns and textures that are simply not possible if you just stick to conventional paving slabs or bricks. Small paving units such as granite sets or their cheaper concrete look-alikes are ideal for mixing and matching with other more natural materials such as pebbles, cobbles and gravel. Reclaimed bricks that weather and crumble have an 'organic' feel suitable for older properties and country settings, but brick pavers, frost-proof quarry tiles and the smallest square and rectangular paving slabs are also useful for mixing together to achieve a mosaic effect. Many features can be laid directly onto a sand base overlaying well-rammed hardcore or firmed earth. But you can also lay into concrete for greater stability and this makes the task of arranging irregular shapes like cobbles into particular patterns much easier. In a small, informal garden, it does not matter if the results are a little jumbled – that just adds character! Don't forget to factor in room for plants, which can further soften and add interesting texture and

above: *Small pebbles laid in curving rows make a finely textured pathway that sets off the plants beautifully.*

colour to a hard surface. Leave out the mortar between paving blocks and brush in sifted soil and sand mixed with the seed of aromatic, drought-tolerant herbs like oregano and *Lavandula angustifolia* 'Munstead'; carpeting and cushion forming alpines such as campanula and thrift and old-fashioned flowers like heartsease (*Viola tricolor*) and the hardy annual, sweet white alyssum.

VARIATIONS ON THE THEME The good thing about small paving units is that you can lay them to fit any shape or awkward space. Within a fairly simply laid patio or pathway you could create square panels containing circular designs – perhaps a spiral or flower motif made from pebbles and cobbles set into concrete. Or you could lay a radiating pattern of bricks or pantiles cut into slices laid like the rays of the sun. Make special flooring features to draw the eye towards a seating area, a garden ornament or a small pool and consider edging plain paving with a patterned border of sets, tiles, bricks or cobbles to lift the whole area.

Do:

• Experiment with mixing and matching all kinds of small hard landscaping materials

• Try out your designs and create a paper template for more complex patterns to refer to as you work

• Use small units to create special paving features and decorative borders or to fill in awkward gaps

• Replace larger paving units with smaller ones for textural interest

Don't:

• Leave path surfaces dangerously uneven

• Make things too complicated or mix in too many diverse materials, or it could make the garden feel too 'busy'

• Fill all the gaps with mortar. Leave spaces so that you can plant into your designs

right: *You can make a most attractive pathway by blending contrasting surfaces, such as gravel and brick, with creeping plants. Creeping thyme is excellent in this situation, as it does not mind being crushed occasionally, and being fragrant, it creates its own pleasant atmosphere.*

Laying pebbles and cobbles

Skill level:

Some DIY experience

required

Best time to do:

Anytime the ground is

not too wet or frozen

Special tools required:

Spirit level; club

hammer; builder's

trowel

Time required:

A whole weekend

WHAT YOU WILL NEED

- Ready-mixed mortar
- Edging material to outline
path, e.g. brick pavers
- Pebbles or cobbles
- Spirit level, club hammer,
builder's trowel
- Straight wooden offcut
- Clear silicone masonry sealant

Naturally rounded pebbles and larger cobblestones are a good way of introducing varieties of shape and texture to your paving. You can use them to create paths and patios, but they are more commonly used as a visual counterpoint to flat surfaces – perhaps as a border or to highlight a garden feature, such as a sundial or statue. Their advantage over other garden paving materials is their relatively small size, which makes it easy to fit them round curves and irregularly shaped obstacles. However, because of this, they do take much longer to lay than other materials. You can buy pebbles and cobblestones from builders' suppliers and garden centres, in a range of sizes and colours. Small quantities – enough for an individual garden feature – are usually sold in bags.

right: *In this tranquil Japanese garden, carefully selected cobbles have been laid flat to give a relatively smooth surface on which to walk. Notice how well this paving works in around the outline of the stone platform, creating a marked contrast in texture.*

USEFUL TIPS

Pebbles and cobblestones are usually laid in mortar, especially if they are going to be walked on or are used to line a watercourse or surround a fountain. But loose pebbles can be used to discourage weed growth and prevent soil erosion in areas of the garden that are in permanent shade. For large areas it is more economical to buy stones loose by weight. Ask your supplier for advice about coverage and have large quantities delivered; otherwise, more than two or three sacks of heavy stones could wreck your vehicle suspension.

LAYING PEBBLES AND COBBLESTONES

As well as random patterning, small pebbles and cobbles can also be laid in
simple designs to form decorative panels within pathways. The stones can also
be sorted by shade, using the different colours to create darker and paler areas.

1 Outline a pebble path with a row of bricks, sets or pavers bedded into a generous layer of mortar and point.

2 Place pebbles on the mortar bed, as close together as possible. Select for size and colour contrast with their neighbours.

3 Use an offcut and a club hammer to tamp down the pebbles into the mortar bed to ensure that they won't work loose.

4 Check that the stones are reasonably level across the surface. If any project too far, tamp them down further.

5 Water enhances the natural colours and textures of pebbles with dramatic effect. Create this look artificially by coating the finished bed with a clear silicone masonry sealant.

VARIATIONS ON THE THEME

An imaginary stream like this is a traditional element of the Zen dry garden or *karesansui*. After contouring the route, lay down landscape material. Carefully overlap flat pebbles or slate shards to create the impression of a flow of water and make the 'banks' of your stream from differently coloured and shaped cobbles and larger rocks or boulders. You could even add a simple wooden bridge to complete the illusion. This clever dry stream effect works well in just about any kind of garden.

Mosaics and pebble patterns

Skill level:

Some craft/design

experience useful

Best time to do:

Any fine spell, avoiding

frosty periods

Special tools required:

Tile cutter, tile

squeegee

Time required:

Could take a whole

weekend

WHAT YOU WILL NEED

• Ready-mix cement
• Tools to lift paving slab and prepare cement base for mosaic
• PVA glue and brush
• Frost- and water-proof tiles; for example, ones suitable for outdoor pools
• Exterior grade tile adhesive and applicator
• Exterior grade tile grout
• Soft nylon bristle brush
• Tile squeegee

You do not have to be artistically gifted to create a floor mosaic. As you can see from the photograph below, simple designs can be striking. Sometimes all you need to do is to use bands of pebbles in contrasting colours, or change the way that pebbles in different areas are orientated. The larger the pebble or cobble, the more rudimentary the design will be unless you are working over a very large area, and that is not recommended for a novice! Start with something quite modest in size and design until you develop the skill and confidence to go onto more complex and challenging pieces.

Keep the design simple, and if possible mark out a scale plan on squared paper so that you have something to refer to as you work. You might choose a chequerboard design, a spiral or a border using the traditional Greek key. To emphasise the garden theme, you could incorporate a simple tulip or daisy motif. A heavenly theme could also work well, with panels showing a stylised sun, moon or star. Or you could go for something more symbolic, such as the Chinese yin and yang

below: *Set within a larger area of paving, this pebble mosaic panel makes a real feature and shows how a very simple design can still be very effective. It is all the more dramatic because of the subtly contrasting colours in the design.*

above right: *This highly original mosaic of bricks, tiles and broken paving is full of character. Although at first sight the design seems random, bricks have been laid to create a flowing curve, suggestive of movement and the blue tiles provide a linking theme.*

symbol. Give these mosaic features the prominence they deserve, siting them at the junction of two pathways, to focus attention on a garden ornament, pool or fountain, or to enhance a seating or outdoor dining area.

For a completely different and wonderfully eccentric and relaxed feel, why not create an abstract design with several different kinds of paving and coloured tiles? You could use broken paving slabs, old bricks, cobbles … in fact any frost-proof materials you have to hand. This really will be an original piece of garden art! Just make it up as you go along, fitting the pieces together like a jigsaw and filling in awkward gaps with pebbles or bits of broken tile. As well as the browns, greys and terracotta colours normally associated with paving, consider adding a dynamic splash of Moroccan blue in the form of glazed tiles.

MAKING A MOSAIC

You can insert small mosaic panels into paths and paved areas. Just lift the required number of paving slabs and, using the existing foundations as a base, pour on a smooth layer of ready-mix cement. Allow this to dry and, to prevent moisture seeping through, seal the surface with PVA. When dry, mark out your design; if you are a beginner, choose a very simple pattern. Make a scaled up drawing and use that to prepare cardboard templates for each of the separate elements. Prepare frost-proof tiles, e.g. suitable for outdoor pools, snipping them with a tile cutter into suitable sizes. Working in quite small areas within the outline of your design, spread a layer of exterior quality adhesive. Then apply the coloured tile pieces section by section, fitting them together like a jigsaw and leaving gaps between. When these are dry, spread over exterior quality, waterproof tiling grout, working it into all the crevices. Then, using a tile squeegee, scrape off the excess to reveal the design.

Garden decks and wooden surfacing

Wood is a material that allows your inventiveness full rein when it comes to creating walkways and sitting areas in a garden. Unlike masonry, it is light and easy to handle and can be worked with simple and familiar tools, allowing you to use it on any scale and in any way you wish. Set alongside a garden pond or other water feature, it conjures up images of sturdy wooden jetties on a boating lake. Placed in the midst of an overflowing border, it creates a natural looking pathway that blends in with the informality of the planting far more sympathetically than a paved path ever could. Raised wooden boardwalks give a different perspective on the garden and blend in beautifully with wild or woodland plantings.

The structures you create with wood can be built *in situ* on a grand scale, or can be assembled from small modules put together in your shed, garage or workshop and then arranged – and rearranged at will – in the garden. Wood really is the most versatile of materials and there are so many different roles for it in the garden – whether practical or aesthetic.

However you decide to use wood, remember the two essential rules. First, all wood that spends its life in contact with the ground must either be a naturally durable species, or else be thoroughly pre-treated with wood preservative to keep rot and insect attack at bay. Go for timber that has been pressure-treated with preservative rather than merely dipped, which is not nearly as effective. Hardwoods such as oak and the tropical iroko are more durable than most softwoods, though western red cedar has a natural resistance to rot. But hardwoods are more expensive and often harder to obtain in the right form and most environmentally aware gardeners now try to steer

above: A sunny deck will warm up quickly so you can walk straight out of the house onto it in bare feet. Create a relaxed 'outdoor room' feel with colourful pots, pebbles and comfortable furniture. Leave the wood natural or use one of the attractively coloured decking treatments to coordinate with your house and garden.

right: Being a natural material, decking makes a perfect partnership with water. Use it to overhang a pool so that it helps to camouflage the lining and brings you into closer contact with the surface of the water.

DECKING TILES

You can buy small, pre-assembled slatted wooden decking tiles made from preservative-treated softwood. Simply lay these on supporting joists to create whatever area of decking you require and screw in position.

clear of tropical hardwoods. Secondly, wood can become slippery when wet, since moss and algae will grow on its surface, so you need to be prepared to scrub it down once or twice a year to keep it in a safe condition and looking good (a high pressure water sprayer is ideal for this task). If possible, avoid building decks and boardwalks in damp, shady areas where they will be prone to moss and rot, and you might want to reconsider using decking in areas of high rainfall. If decking is persistently slippery, cover it with galvanised wire mesh to improve the tread. This is also a good idea for ensuring the safety of bridges and boardwalks over water.

Do:

• Consider using reclaimed timber for decking as it already has a weathered look and can be a cheap way to obtain durable hardwoods
• Keep decking dry attaching it to joists supported on brick or breezeblock piers bedded in the subsoil
• Paint with natural or coloured decking preservative

Don't:

• Allow moss and algae to build up as it can make decking dangerously slippery. In damp, shady areas cover with galvanized chicken wire
• Use untreated wood. Buy pressure-treated decking timber which will resist rot for up to ten years
• Forget about lighting! Recessed uplighters are easier to install if you prepare the holes before the deck is in place

Constructing wooden decking

Wooden decking is a natural alternative to hard paving in formal and informal gardens. The raw material is widely available and costs broadly the same as paving (unless you choose an exotic hardwood instead of softwood). It is much easier to cut to size than paving slabs or blocks, quickly blends in with its surroundings as it weathers and is more forgiving to walk or sit down on than hard paving. The only disadvantages of wooden decking are that it will need occasional maintenance work and that it can be slippery in wet weather. Make sure that all the sawn joists and planed planks for decking have been pretreated with preservative and apply a preservative stain to the completed structure, paying special attention to any cut ends you have sawn during construction. To keep the decking clear of damp ground and reduce the incidence of rot, set the joists on bricks, ideally with a pad of damp-proof membrane or roofing felt between bricks and joists. Clear the ground beneath the decking and apply a long-term weedkiller first.

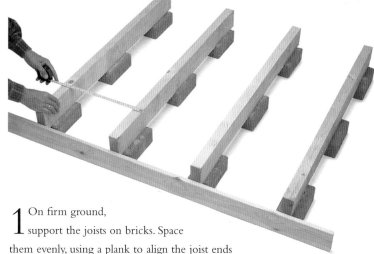

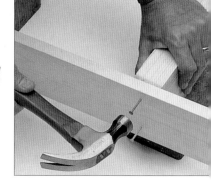

1 On firm ground, support the joists on bricks. Space them evenly, using a plank to align the joist ends and to check that the tops are level. If you construct decking in small, self-contained units like this, you can work under cover.

2 Cut a fascia board to the width of the decking and secure it to the joist ends with galvanised nails. Fix a batten across the tops of the joists at the other end of the deck.

Decking looks particularly good in modern surroundings teamed with architectural plants like yucca, grasses, phormium and the Chusan palm. It also complements woodland gardens. In dappled shade, continue the timber theme with wooden furniture and plant hostas, hardy ferns, camellias and compact rhododendrons in wooden half barrels. And, for an oriental feel, choose dwarf pines, irregularly shaped junipers, weeping conifers and bamboos.

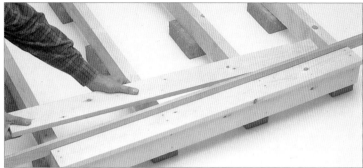

3 Cut and position the first plank across the joists so that its front edge projects over the fascia and forms a projecting nosing. Secure it to each joist with two nails, making it good and solid.

4 Leave a slight gap between adjacent planks so that rainwater can drain freely. Set a slim batten against the first plank, then position the second plank against the batten. A temporary batten on the other side holds the joists parallel while you fix the planks. The gaps not only allow rain water to disperse and air to flow through and dry the timber, it also lets light in, so you must make sure that the ground below cannot sprout weeds.

5 Secure the plank to each joist, punching two galvanised nails just below the wood surface. A string line will help to align the nail heads across the decking.

6 Set the decking on bricks or blocks bedded in the subsoil so that the joists are held clear of the ground. Hide the supports with pebbles or low-level planting.

Wooden decking makes a natural background to many plants and sets off containers perfectly.

above: *Wooden decking can extend to cover as large an area as you need and it is relatively simple to introduce a little design flair. Here planks are laid at an angle to the house wall. A shallow step, rotated at a different angle, goes down to the gravel path below and stylishly accommodates the gentle slope of the site. The overall effect is entirely in keeping with the deck's surroundings.*

Decorative effects with decking

Skill level:

DIY and carpentry

experience required

Best time to do:

Anytime when the

weather is dry

Special tools required:

Hammer; combination

square; panel saw

Time required:

At least one whole

weekend, if not more

WHAT YOU WILL NEED

• Timber for joists, planking and edging battens
• Slim batten as a spacing guide
• Hammer, panel saw, sander, combination square, tape measure
• Galvanised nails
• Preservative and brushes
• Bricks or blocks to support joists plus damp-proof membrane to separate brick supports from joists
• Ready-mix concrete to provide foundations for the piers

Since wood is easy to cut to size and shape, you can create any number of decorative designs. Carefully work out the design on paper first, adjusting the spacing between the planks to ensure that a whole number will fit the area you want to cover. You can create chevron and diamond patterns by reversing the direction of the planking on adjacent areas of the decking. To protect bare feet in summer, make sure that all the cut ends are free from splinters and round off the edges slightly with sandpaper. Provide additional protection for the perimeter of the decking by nailing on edge battens all round and work in plenty of preservative to the cut ends when you come to paint the deck on completion. For a keen DIYer with experience of woodworking, all manner of other designs are possible. For example, you could create a gently curving leading edge that follows the contours of the garden or a series of semi-circular steps.

1 Use preservative-treated sawn softwood for joists. Space them evenly and nail a transverse joist to their ends to hold them in place.

2 To set planks at a 45° angle to the joists, use a combination square to position the first plank at the corner of the joist framework.

3 Once you have positioned the first plank accurately, remove the square and mark the plank position on the joists below.

4 Use the square with its 45° face against the plank edge to mark a guideline for the nails above the centre line of the joist beneath.

5 Nail on the first plank. Drive in the nail nearest the corner first, check alignment with pencil lines and secure with two more nails.

6 Use a slim batten as a spacing guide to ensure that the gaps between adjacent boards are the same across the decking surface.

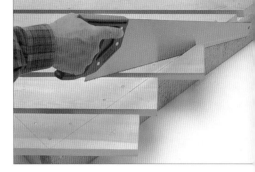

7 Repeat the procedure with the square and pencil to ensure that the nails securing the second plank are in line with those holding the first one.

8 Use the spacer batten to position subsequent planks, nailing them to the joists one by one. Punch the nail heads just below the surface of the wood.

9 When all the planks are nailed down, place a straightedge over the projecting ends, align it with the outer face of the joist below and mark a cutting line.

10 Use a panel saw to cut off the projecting ends of the planks. Saw just on the waste side of the cutting line, taking care to keep the saw blade vertical as you work.

PRESERVING WOOD

Wood stains and preservatives come in many shades. Look out for those specifically targeted at decking which both preserve and

stain. Colour your decking to coordinate with planting schemes or to create a particular atmosphere. Soft blues are gentle on the eye and work well with most flower colours. White is pure and simple, and black is dramatic and Oriental looking.

11 Sand all the cut ends of the planks to remove splinters or nails on edging battens for a neat finish and to protect the exposed end grain against rot and damage.

12 You can treat the finished decking with clear wood preservative (as here), a coloured preservative stain or wood dye. Avoid varnish, which will soon blister and crack.

Support the joists on brick piers

Smooth off any splinters by sanding

Edging battens give the decking a neat finish

Vertical Gardening

Without the vertical structures that surround our gardens and create enclosures within them, the space would feel very exposed as well as flat and rather boring. What is more, we would have nowhere to grow any of the beautiful climbers and wall shrubs that nature has to offer. Where space is at a premium, growing upwards can make a lot of sense. Most climbers and wall-trained shrubs take up little room, thus allowing for more plants to be grown at their feet. With vertical gardening we have the opportunity to study the form of foliage and flower at eye level or in the case of scented blooms, at nose level! But even without planting, vertical elements like fencing and trelliswork can be highly decorative in their own right and contribute greatly to the style or feel of the garden that they embellish.

Garden dividers

The walls, fences and hedges that surround the garden serve different purposes. Firstly and perhaps most importantly, they define the space. They also provide security from unwanted intrusion onto the 'territory'. The green 'walls' of the garden room allow us to relax and enjoy the privacy of our own particular Eden. They can also help to create shelter in more exposed areas so that the garden has a microclimate amenable for plants as well as its human inhabitants. Walls, fences and trellis panels provide support for climbers and wall shrubs, allowing a completely different set of plants to be cultivated alongside their ground-based neighbours.

below: *Fences can become features in their own right. This picket fence has a very distinctive style due to the shaping of its wooden slats.*

Do:

• Choose boundaries and dividers that suit the style of your house and garden
• Use trellis to create inner garden 'rooms'
• Utilise the vertical garden space by attaching a support framework for climbers and wall shrubs
• Make small gardens feel bigger by disguising the boundaries

Don't:

• Mix too many styles or materials when making boundaries and divisions
• Allow hedges to get out of hand. Over a certain height, they become unmanageable and cut out too much light. And if they grow too wide they rob the garden of valuable planting space
• Erect totally solid boundaries in very exposed areas. This can create even more turbulence and damage garden plants

left: *Trellis panels make effective dividers within the garden, creating extra shelter and privacy and separating areas with a different style or atmosphere. These square trellis panels with finials crowning each of the posts help to create an air of elegance. Diamond-pattern trellis and panels create a more informal look. You can now buy trellis with 'windows' or attractively shaped apertures to provide 'glimpsed views' through to the adjacent garden.*

below left: *A simple and rather rustic-looking post and rail fence marks the boundary of this garden but will probably be removed once the hedge has thickened out. A fence like this can be a good deterrent for preventing people from taking short cuts through a newly planted hedge and creating unsightly gaps as a result.*

In larger plots, it may be possible to subdivide the area into a series of smaller and more intimate 'rooms' using various kinds of screen. These don't have to be very substantial – trellis panels are ideal. They baffle the eye, without completely blocking the view and help make the space feel more light and airy.

Hedges create living boundaries and can be formal or informal depending on what plants are used and how often they are clipped, if at all. It is important to choose the right material for a hedge because it could end up looking out of place. Hedges can take up quite a lot of space, especially when they are not clipped and also rob the ground of nutrients affecting nearby plantings.

Overhead structures in the garden

far right: Shaped trellis has been attached to this small pergola to create a feature backdrop for the border. Being symmetrical the effect is quite formal though pretty and romantic. Clematis 'Ville de Lyon' takes centre stage.

below: An archway covered in Clematis montana *frames the statue at the end of the pathway beautifully. Notice how the arch is bedded into the framework of the garden.*

There is something wonderfully evocative about sitting beneath a canopy of foliage on a hot summer's day, the light filtering through softly. It is as though the garden is cocooning you. You can achieve this effect with trees, but there is not always room, especially in very small gardens. The other possibility to create a similar effect is to build some kind of overhead structure to support climbers, for example a decorative metal arbour erected over a seat or a wooden pergola built over an outdoor dining area. Overhead structures effectively form the ceiling of your outdoor room. They can consist of a very light framework but they still have that same psychological effect, making us feel enclosed, safe and secure, and therefore at the same time more relaxed.

Archways are inherently romantic and can be used to mark passage into a different area of the garden and to create a sense of mystery. They can also be used in a theatrical way to frame a view or a garden feature. Pergolas built over a section of pathway have a similar function and can also help to create a contrasting atmosphere along a garden walkway – outside the tunnel, the garden feels open, warm and sunny; inside, cool, shady and enclosed.

Whatever kind of overhead structure you choose to construct in your garden, always ensure – as with any garden feature – that it will complement your existing garden design and tie in well with the house and any other structures nearby. Scale is the main consideration with an inherently tall, upright feature: too large an arbour or archway will look ridiculous in a very small town garden whereas a mini pergola will look equally out of place in the garden of a sprawling country spread.

right: *Climber-covered archways can help to create an air of mystery. Here the view is framed by a large-leaved ivy, making the sunny flower-filled area beyond all the more enticing.*

Do:

• Use pergolas to create an easy transition between house and garden

• Build pergolas to create 'outdoor rooms' suitable for alfresco dining

• Use archways to define passage into different areas of the garden

• Use archways and covered walkways to create vistas and highlight focal points in the garden

• Make a secret sitting area beneath a climber-covered arbour so that you can 'escape' now and then!

Don't:

• Make pergolas and archways too low or narrow. Build vertical and overhead structures in the correct proportions so that the space they occupy feels comfortable and not claustrophobic. Build for a solid and substantial feel

• Place archways in isolation. Fit them into the garden layout in a meaningful and logical way, e.g. to mark a gap in the border or fence

• Plant vigorous climbers on small structures; they will eventually be swamped!

Climbing plants for decorative effects

below: Here an old fashioned looking English rose has been trained to cover a large bare wall. Rambler roses, or climbers with rambler blood in them, are wonderful for covering large areas quickly but may not be repeat flowering. Check carefully before buying.

Climbers and wall shrubs are invaluable because of the speed with which they can cover bare walls and fences, softening the hard lines. Because of their flexible stems and upward growth habit, climbers allow you to fit potentially large plants into a small space. By growing tall climbing roses, honeysuckle and clematis over arches and pergolas, it is possible to coil the long stems around the uprights and 'concertina' them into a smaller space. This technique also makes them flower better, since more of the stems are close to the horizontal, and thus form more flower buds. And training large shrubs, such as pyracantha and fremontodendron or evergreen ceanothus, flat against a wall is

Do:

• Make use of scented climbers like honeysuckle, jasmine and *Trachelospermum asiaticum* around doorways and garden seats
• Use vigorous climbers like Russian vine, Virginia creeper and the Kiftsgate rose *only* to camouflage unsightly garden buildings and to cover large structures rapidly
• Combine climbers with a similar pruning regime to make maintenance easier

Don't:

• Forget to provide adequate support for climbers and wall shrubs and to tie in new growth
• Neglect to check and loosen old plant ties that could be damaging the plant
• Plant climbers right next to a wall or fence. Angle the plant in towards the wall

left: *You can train climbers around a doorway to create a romantic or cottage garden feel. Here the bell-shaped blooms of* Clematis tangutica *combine with* Clematis 'Perle d'Azur'. *Both can be hard-pruned, but with vigorous growers like these you may still need to do a lot of cutting back in summer to keep the access clear and more compact alternatives might be considered.*

often the only way to accommodate them. They are also much easier to manage. However, in general, the more naturally compact types of climber, and those that can be successfully pruned, are the easiest to cope with. Passionflower (*Passiflora caerulea*) and the Viticella types of clematis are both excellent because they can be hard pruned each spring without sacrificing summer flowers. Check the ultimate size before buying. This is vital with climbing or rambler roses, as some grow to be huge.

Spectacular plants for stunning effects

above: *A vine's decorative foliage and grapes add a Mediterranean flavour to a pergola. Choose a variety suitable for fruiting outdoors in your locality.*

Climbers produce some of the biggest and most sensational flowers in the garden. Wisteria is a favourite, with its huge 'bunch of grape'-shaped early summer flowers in purple or white. Normally grown on a house front, it does need frequent attention as vigorous shoots can grow behind gutters or drainpipes forcing the fixtures away from the wall. Proper pruning prevents this problem and also encourages this notoriously slow-to-flower climber to begin blooming. The quicker you curb its spread, the sooner this will happen. Always buy named cultivars grafted onto a rootstock.

For a hot sunny spot, even if the soil tends to be a bit dry (a problem close to a wall, since the brickwork deflects rainwater) then passion flower (*Passiflora caerulea*) and trumpet vines (*Campsis radicans*, the more tender *C.grandiflora* or the hardier hybrid between the two *C.* × *tagliabuana*) are good choices. Both have spectacular flowers and are tougher than their exotic looks would suggest. For scent, the climbing jasmines, *Jasminum officinale* or *J.* × *stephanense* are hard to beat. On a pergola or arch they team up perfectly with roses, but are also a useful way to add scent to more spectacular but perfume-free flowers. Trachelospermum is also fragrant, and like jasmine and honeysuckle will twine up vertical training wires and trellis unaided. Many of the large-flowered hybrid clematis also produce spectacular displays, rivalling any of their more exotic counterparts. Grow where the roots can be shaded and top growth is in the sun. Exceptions are the large white-flowered clematis like 'Marie Boisselot', and the pink and white striped varieties such as 'Nelly Moser', which prefer shelter from strong sunlight.

Climbers that change their leaf colour with the seasons add an extra decorative dimension. Examples of plants that can produce fiery autumn tints include the Virginia creepers (*Parthenocissus*) and the vine *Vitis coignetiae*, which has giant, tropical looking leaves.

above: *The surprisingly hardy passion flower (*Passiflora caerulea*) has exotic blooms followed by orange plum-shaped fruits and climbs via tendrils.*

The exciting pink leaved kiwi, *Actinidia kolomikta*, develops its best colouration in full sun, whereas the golden hop (*Humulus lupulus* 'Aureus'), an herbaceous climber of great vigour, thrives in light shade and really makes the area glow. Prune back almost to ground level in spring and remove old growth.

Do:

• Look around your neighbourhood and visit local parks and botanic gardens to give you an idea about whether you could grow something a little more exotic and out of the ordinary
• Use exotic-looking but moderately hardy climbers for sunny sheltered aspects including, passion flower, *C. × tagliabuana* 'Madame Galen' , jasmines, red- and orange-flowered honeysuckles, the potato vine *Solanum crispum* 'Glasnevin' and *S. laxum* 'Album'
• Experiment with growing unusual climbers from seed including annuals like the cup and saucer vine *Cobaea scandens*

Don't:

• Buy unnamed wisteria plants growing on their own roots. Though cheaper, these are almost certainly seed-raised and may never flower
• Allow wisteria to continue to grow beyond a rigidly allotted space. If you do you may continue to wait for flower buds to appear. Consider growing plants as spectacular weeping standards in pots
• Rely on deciduous climbers and wall shrubs for wall and fence coverage, especially those which are dubiously hardy. Mix in a few tough evergreens. English ivy varieties (*Hedera helix*) will weave in with all kinds of wall plantings and the large leaved *Hedera colchica* 'Sulphur Heart' makes a bold feature

above: *The vivid red leaves of the vigourous climber* Parthenocissus tricuspidata *(Boston ivy), make a stunning show in the autumn, but they can blow away in a single storm. All Virginia creepers are deciduous, so be prepared for a large expanse of bare stems and walls during the winter months, once the plants have died back.*

left: *The potato vine* Solanum crispum *'Glasnevin' is a spectacular climber. The clusters of curiously shaped purple flowers are produced over a long period. Use it to add an exotic touch to a warm wall or trellis structure. There is a lovely white species available, named* S. laxum *'Album'.*

A rustic sweet pea wigwam

Rustic willow plant supports are fun and fashionable. They are available ready-made, sold by craftspeople from their stands at flower shows or by mail order direct from their studios. A limited range is sometimes available in garden centres, too. The basic material is versatile and easy to work with, so provided you can find a source of willow stems or have long flexible prunings from plants like coloured-stemmed dogwoods, you can create your own designs. The long, slender, one-year-old willow stems (correctly called withies) are sometimes available in winter by mail order from basket makers in willow-growing regions (look for advertisements in craft or gardening magazines).

1 Choose a container heavy enough to support a tall structure. Fill it with potting mix and push an odd number of tall, straight willow wands evenly around the edge to form the uprights of the plant support.

2 Take a prepared willow wand and tie the thick end firmly to one of the uprights above the rim of the pot. Weave the wand in and out between the uprights, keeping the uprights evenly spaced. Once the first wand is in place; press the layers close together to tighten the weave. Tie or tuck in the loose end.

3 Weave in a second wand as before. Continually check that the uprights remain evenly spaced; it takes a long time to put things right later on if you overlook this essential monitoring. To neaten the thin end of the withy, hook it round an upright, bend it back in the opposite direction and tuck it into the weave, down the edge of an upright.

4 Only tie in the first withy. Then weave in new stems leaving a long 'tail' inside. When both bands are complete, cut off the excess stems with secateurs.

5 Gather together the tops of the uprights and tie them well with strong string. Do not worry if this looks untidy; it will be hidden by a decorative willow covering later on.

6 Take a very thin, flexible piece of willow 60-90cm(24-36in) long, and push it down between the tops of the stems. If the string is secure, it should be a tight fit. Bind the new piece of willow around this section, working neatly from bottom to top and secure.

right: *Plant a short-growing sweet pea mixture such as 'Jet Set', which will be in scale with the support and should not need much tying in.*

Planting a clematis obelisk

Skill level:

Beginner gardener

Best time to do:

Late spring/early

summer – as soon as

fresh stock comes into

the garden centres

Special tools required:

None

Time required:

Allow a couple of hours

WHAT YOU WILL NEED

- Flat pack trellis obelisk kit
- Matching Versailles planter with drainage in the form of gravel
- Large-flowered, late blooming clematis hybrid or one of the Viticella hybrids – any that take hard pruning to keep in bounds
- Potting mix
- Trowel

A good way of growing climbers is on a framework that stands in the pot itself. Of the annual climbers, canary creeper (*Tropaeolum peregrinum*), cup-and-saucer vine (*Cobaea scandens*), morning glory (*Ipomoea*), Chilean glory vine (*Eccremocarpus*) and sweet peas are all good choices. But if you want a climber that can be left in the same container for several years, a clematis is ideal and a trellis obelisk makes an elegant support. All climbers in pots need

1 Carefully remove the clematis from its pot, with the cane still supporting the stem. Ease the clematis and cane into the tub. Add potting mix to within 5cm(2in) of the top of the tub; firm down. About 5cm(2in) of the stem should be buried.

2 Remove the cane. Set up the trellis as instructed, working the legs of the obelisk into the tub without disturbing the plant rootball.

3 Space the stems around the support. Tie them in loosely to prevent them becoming trapped in between the trellis panels.

Clematis *'Hagley Hybrid'. Tie in new growth regularly to maintain a good shape, and remove dead flowers.*

4 As a finishing touch to the feature, put the finial in place over the tapered ends of the wood. This secures the panels into a pyramid shape. Water thoroughly and keep compost moist but not wet.

left: *Obelisks are one of the smartest ways of raising interest in borders. This one shows off* Clematis *'Madame Julia Correvon', a late-flowering cultivar.*

CLEMATIS IN POTS AROUND THE GARDEN

Stand a large tub of clematis at the base of a wall and let the plant climb up supports. Or encourage the stems to grow up pergola poles, providing grip by tacking clematis mesh loosely round the uprights. You can also use wire topiary frames – wind the stems round from base to top and back again.

above: *Stand a tub of clematis at the base of a wall with an existing climber trained out over it, and the clematis will cling to the framework of stems.*

frequent watering and generous feeding. Start two weeks after planting in the tub, using a liquid or soluble tomato feed to encourage flowering. After a few weeks, alternate this with a general-purpose feed. Although most annual climbers are real sunlovers, clematis prefer cool conditions at the roots. In a sunny spot, stand other containers around them so that their foliage shades the soil and the base of the plant. Prune clematis in pots as if they were growing in the garden; pruning strategies vary from one variety to another, so keep the instructions that come on the plant label. After three years, tip the plant carefully out of its pot in early spring before it starts growing, carefully shake off the old soil and repot the clematis back into the same tub or one that is a size larger, using fresh potting mix.

Growing climbers against a wall

Trellis panels are available in a wide variety of styles and materials. Trellis framework is attractive in its own right and its impact can be accentuated by painting it in different colours. Try a soft blue, jade green, lavender or even a bright yellow water-based wood stain or paint that doubles as a timber preservative. Natural wood finish and white are traditional choices, the latter conveying a 'classic' style to the garden. You can fix trellis panels to free-standing posts to create simple 'walls' that climbers can clothe with foliage and flowers, or you can build up arches, arbours, bowers and pergolas to suit your space and budget.

left: *Expandable cedar trellis panels need support. Try screwing them to cedar stakes on the wall.*

right: *Use soft string to tie honey-suckle stems to a trellis panel or a cane. The stems are delicate so take care when handling them and tie knots loosely.*

WHAT YOU WILL NEED

- Trellis panel (pre-stained or painted)
- Wooden battens
- Screws and wall plugs
- Electric hammer action drill with masonry bit
- Screwdriver
- Climber (pre-soaked)
- Well-rotted compost or manure
- Watering can or hose to water in after planting

above: *A wooden trellis panel with the horizontal battens fixed directly to the wall. This leaves the vertical pieces free, but shoots will not be able to twine around the cross pieces.*

above: *Turn the panel round and the cross pieces form a series of rungs held away from the wall by the vertical battens. This might be better for roses that are trained horizontally.*

above: *The best approach is to attach it onto stout battens that keep the whole panel away from the surface. This gives maximum support for the climber and leaves a healthy air gap behind.*

GIVING CLIMBERS THE BEST START

Avoid the dry zone at the base of a wall. Dig a large planting hole about 45cm (18in) away from the wall, incorporating plenty of well-rotted organic matter, and soak the rootball of the plant in a bucket of water. If necessary, undo the shoots from their cane and re-tie the main shoot to a

VARIATIONS ON THE THEME

For a more subtle look than trellis, use galvanized or green plastic coated training wire to form a grid-like support framework that is barely visible on brickwork, so ideal for

above: Clematis *'Jackmanii' is one of the larger hybrids, here adding a purple background to the red blooms of* Phlox *'Starfire' and the emerging white flowers of* Sedum spectabile.

covering house walls where trellis may be inappropriate. Tap vine-eyes into mortar with a hammer or, to avoid damage, use screw types that fix into pre-drilled holes fitted with wall plugs. Set 1.8m (6ft) apart with a separation of 45 cm(18in) between the horizontals. Secure one end and thread the wire trough the vine eyes, pulling it taught. Once the horizontals are in place, attach the verticals. Check that all wires are taut and fully secure.

longer cane to reach the wall. Alternatively, fan out the stems of the climber, attaching them to a series of canes. Plant the climber at an angle so that the tip of the cane touches the wall (see above).

Classic climbers for shade

WHAT YOU WILL NEED

• Trellis panel attached to wall just above the height of the Versailles planter
• Versailles planter or large pot with matching feet
• Healthy honeysuckle plant with good root system and several stems branching from the base
• Gravel and crocks for drainage
• Soil-based potting mix. This is preferable for long-term planting
• Trowel

Plain green ivy is phenomenally shade-tolerant. Varieties of Hedera helix *(English ivy) have leaves in a bewildering array of shapes and variegations.* And when plants mature, they can produce very different 'adult' foliage as well as insignificant flowers. Ivy is self-clinging and has a reputation for damaging brickwork, but it is only a problem when pulled off already crumbling mortar. Slow at first, by its third year it begins to grow vigorously. Keep within the required boundaries by regular pruning and do not let it grow over wooden window and doorframes or into guttering. Honeysuckle is another classic shade plant, this time grown mainly for its flowers, though in some cases the foliage is evergreen. *Lonicera periclymenum* 'Belgica' and *L. p.* 'Serotina' (early and late Dutch honeysuckles) are commonly grown, having a wonderful perfume and twining habit.

above: *The yellow edges and irregular yellow patches on the attractive leaves distinguish* Hedera helix *'Marginata Major' from other varieties. The late flowers provide food for insects.*

far right: *The beautiful apricot yellow flowers of* Lonicera × tellmanniana *make a good colour match with the marjoram and poppies as they grow together on a dry stone wall.*

DIVIDING IVY

A pot of ivy from the garden centre is made up of several rooted cuttings that are easy to split and replant where you want them.

Knock the ivy out of its pot and pull the plantlets apart, taking care not to damage the roots too much in the process. Replant them without delay. You can divide the original plant into ten or more separate rooted cuttings that you can plant in small groups to fill particular spaces.

PLANTING A HONEYSUCKLE IN A TUB

Honeysuckles are universal favourites and there are many different species and cultivars to choose from. They can be grown in a variety of ways: in hedgerows, up trees, as pillars or as specimens in a tub with a trellis support.

1 Fill the tub with potting mixture and make a hole for the rootball, allowing about 5cm(2in) of soil below the roots.

2 Place the plant – with its cane – into the planting hole, without losing too much of the soil adhering to the roots.

3 Gently firm in the soil to eliminate air spaces. Add more potting mix if necessary, but leave space for watering. Use soft string to tie the individual climbing stems.

4 Give the honeysuckle a generous watering and then keep the plant moist to encourage its establishment.

Making a feature with climbing roses

Skill level:

Beginner gardener

Best time to do:

Autumn through to late

spring, during a mild

spell and whenever the

ground is not frozen

Special tools required:

None

Time required:

Up to an hour

WHAT YOU WILL NEED

- Climbing rose
- Well-rotted manure or organic soil conditioner, plus some slow-release fertiliser containing trace elements
- Digging spade, border fork and trowel or small border spade
- Bamboo cane to check planting depth
- Soft twine to tie in shoots

Both ramblers and climbers make quality contributions to the garden, not only because they have large and abundant flowers, superb colours and, in some cases, scent and a repeat-flowering habit, but because they add both a vertical and a horizontal dimension. Ramblers like 'Rambling Rector' and 'Seagull' create an old-fashioned country or cottage garden look and can be extremely vigorous, perhaps reaching up into trees or covering the roof of a shed. Modern hybrid climbing roses such as 'Compassion' and 'Golden Showers' have sturdier stems, may be more resistant to mildew and bear larger flowers in smaller trusses than ramblers. Many are repeat flowering too, whereas ramblers often have just one spectacular show of blooms. When building a rose feature such as an arbour, archway or even a large pergola walkway such as the one illustrated, it is

CHOOSING A CLIMBING ROSE

Choose a moderate climber for walls or restricted spaces. A more vigorous variety is needed on a fence. Most climbers or ramblers will grow on a pergola. Choose a fast-growing variety to grow into a tree.

1 Dig a hole about 30cm(12in) across and deep. Make sure the hole is at the centre of the trellis and not to one side.

2 Fork well-rotted organic matter into the excavated soil and base of the hole, making sure it is well mixed in.

3 Plant the rose, using a cane to check the depth. If you haven't used manure, work in some soil conditioner and slow-release fertilizer.

4 Firm in the soil to eliminate any air pockets, which can interfere with root development. Water in well.

5 Spread out the branches, even though they are short, and tie in the shoots to the trellis with soft string and a simple knot.

important to choose the right plants for the job. Roses with the right habit to match with your style of garden and which have the appropriate vigour.

The differences in the way that climbing roses grow affects the way in which you prune them. The modern hybrids flower from old wood, which makes them easier to manage and some need little pruning. Ramblers flower from new growth and all old wood must be cut back to a suitable bud in winter. Encouraging a newly planted rose to cover a wall or trellis will occupy the mind while you consider which stems to cut out. However, clearing out dead wood will help to keep these decisions to a minimum.

above: *This spectacular pergola walkway made from rustic poles must be heaven to walk beneath in summer with the fragrance of all those blooms. Choose roses with sufficient vigour to climb up and over the pergola and which have good disease resistance and preferably a repeat flowering habit, for example 'The New Dawn'. Extend the season of interest with the rose's natural partner, clematis.*

Creating privacy with fence and trellis panels

Skill level:

DIY experience useful

Best time to do:

Anytime in fine

weather, provided the

ground is not too dry

and hard or

waterlogged

Special tools required:

Striking block; mallet;

spirit level

Time required:

A whole weekend

WHAT YOU WILL NEED

- Fencing post spike (this can be driven into the ground or with very stony ground, set into a hole filled with concrete
- Striking block (can be hired) and mallet
- Fence post
- Spirit level
- Fence panels or trellis panels
- Fixing clips and screws or nails
- Hammer
- Bricks for temporary support

Whatever type of screening you erect, you must ensure that the supporting posts are secure. Traditionally, part of the post was buried in the ground and anchored with a collar of concrete, but because the base of the post was below ground level, it eventually rotted, even if the wood was treated with preservative. On the other hand, a steel fence spike (and its close relative, the bolt-down fence support designed for use on hard-surfaced areas) keeps the vulnerable post completely above ground level. Both types have a square socket into which you fit the post end and come in sizes to accept 50mm(2in), 75mm(3in) and 100mm(4in) posts. Some have a socket with steel teeth that lock the post permanently in place as it is hammered in. Others have a bolt-operated clamping action reinforced by screws or nails. This system allows you to remove the post without disturbing the socket.

FIXING TO CONCRETE

To secure a bolt-down fence support, drill out each fixing hole to the required depth. Separate the bolt and washer from the anchor sleeve and push the sleeve into the fixing hole with the expanding plug at the bottom. Check that the support is level. Stand the fence support over the fixing holes and drop in the four bolts. Tighten bolts firmly to expand anchor fully.

1 Push the spike into the ground at the required post position. Place the striking block in the socket and start to hammer in the spike.

2 Regularly check that the spike is being driven in precisely vertically, by holding a spirit level against two adjacent faces of the socket in turn. Drive the spike in with repeated hammer blows until the base of the socket is at ground level. Then hammer the post into the socket.

3 Use your spirit level again to check that the post is vertical. If it is not, try tapping the socket sideways to correct the post's tendency to lean.

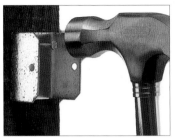

1 On low panels, nail or screw U-shaped metal fixing clips to the inner face.

2 Support the fence panel on bricks or wood to hold it clear of the ground. Slide the edge of the panel into place.

3 Site the next fence post close to the first panel, allowing clearance for the clips. Make sure that the fence spike is vertical and on line as you drive it in.

4 Attach the fence clips to the second post, level with the first. Stand the post in its socket and hammer or clamp it into place. Nail through the fixing clips.

above: *Trellis panels are easy to erect once the posts are in place and a couple set at right angles and smothered in climbers can create a secluded sitting area. They can also fill in a timber framework, for example a pergola.*

left: *To help prevent rotting, keep the soil away from the base of the panel by leaving a gap. You can also put a layer of free-draining gravel beneath each panel to prevent mud splash.*

Constructing a picket fence

Skill level:

Some experience of

woodworking and

joinery an advantage

Best time to do:

Anytime

Special tools required:

Combination square

Time required:

May take the whole

weekend, depending

on the size of the

project

WHAT YOU WILL NEED

• Pre-cut pickets from timber or builders merchant
• Wooden batten to act as a spacer and another to act as a base-board
• Combination square and steel tape measure
• Hammer and galvanized nails, or screws, drill and screwdriver for stronger construction
• Decorative microporous paint or stain and brushes

The design of picket, or paling, fences is based upon medieval palisades, which were formed by driving pointed stakes into the ground to create a simple defensive barrier in battle or to pen in livestock. Picket fences now have a strong association with traditional cottage gardens, especially if painted white, although soft blue or brighter shades are being used with increasing frequency, especially for children's gardens. Set against the backdrop of a hedge the pattern of a picket fence really stands out, but the structure is not as secure as conventional fencing and offers little privacy or protection from prevailing winds. The quickest way to construct the panels is to nail the pickets to the rails, but screws make for a more solid construction. Attach panels to the posts using simple wooden cleats around the ends of the rails.

TIP

Always be sure to use wood that has been pretreated with preservative, since the exposed endgrain is vulnerable to rot. Microporous paint or stain allows the wood to breathe.

right: *Simple pointed pickets are fine but you can make more elaborate shapes (see page 122). To reduce the work involved in creating fancy shapes, make a master template first then cut the marked-out copies with a power saw, jig saw or router.*

below: *This picket fence makes a lovely backdrop to a riotous cottage-style border of hardy annual flowers.*

Picket, or paling, fences are made up as separate panels by nailing precut pickets to two or three horizontal rails, which are then fixed to their supporting posts so that the lower ends of the pickets are held clear of the ground. They are usually about 900mm(3ft) high and commonly used to fence front gardens, where appearance is a more important consideration than high security. The look is very 'country garden'.

1 Use a spacer to set the distance between pickets. Leave a gap between the first picket and the post; check that the picket is square to the rails using a combination square or fixed right angle.

2 Leave the spacer in place as you drive in the nails to ensure that each picket is parallel with the previous one. A base board acts as a handy guide to keep the pickets level during fixing.

3 Support the completed panel on blocks between the posts. Nail the rails to the posts. Their ends should align with the centre of the post. For stronger panels, use screws.

Fencing for the country-style garden

Ranch-style fencing, as its name implies, originated on cattle ranches, where its simple construction was sufficient to keep stock securely penned in at minimal cost. It consists of widely spaced horizontal rails fixed to sturdy posts, and is often used as an inexpensive alternative to picket fencing around front gardens, where marking the boundary line is more important than having a high degree of privacy or security. On low fences, two rails are sufficient, but three or more can be used on higher fences. Ranch-style fences are seldom built more than about 1.2m(4ft) high, since the extra height would not improve either their looks or their security and would increase the cost of the materials unnecessarily. They are often painted white, but if you want a less visually intrusive fence you can use natural shades of green or brown instead. Whatever colour you choose, you can substantially reduce the need for regular redecoration by using a microporous paint or stain. You can improve the security of a ranch-style fence – say, to keep pets in – by fitting an extra rail just above ground level and then stapling on unobtrusive wire mesh between the rails and posts. If you want more privacy and shelter from the prevailing winds than an open ranch-style fence can provide, simply space the rails more closely and fix them alternately to the front and back of the posts.

1 On level ground, fix one end of each rail at the correct level with a single nail or screw. Check for level with a spirit level. When the rail is horizontal, drive in the other fixings to secure both ends of the rail to the posts.

2 Cutting the post tops to a 45° angle helps rainwater to run off and reduces the risk of the fence posts rotting. If you prefer square post tops, you could fit post caps, but these will not drain off so effectively and are more likely to rot.

3 Drive the fixings fully home to secure the rail to the post. Screws are better than nails, providing a firmer fixing than nails, which could be knocked out by heavy impacts. An electric screwdriver will make the job easier.

NATURAL BOUNDARIES

Natural materials are fast becoming favourites for informal fencing panels, as an alternative to traditional woven timber strips. Natural panels last from five to ten years; less in a very windy site, but longer if the panels are firmly fixed and treated with a suitable preservative. Panels can be used permanently or temporarily to protect new shrubs or while a hedge grows. Many different types are available, or you can make a very rustic-looking kind yourself from hazel twigs, bamboo canes or peasticks.

right: *Long strands of dried heather stapled together make attractive and long-lasting russet-toned panels. Though more expensive than many forms of fencing panel, these are very robust and make a superb background to plants.*

above: *Bamboo canes or a mixture of canes and straight, slender willow wands, as here, make a striking and unusual fence panel. Sticks can be left natural or treated with water-based stains to colour them. For a novel effect, group canes of different colours.*

above: *Traditional sheep hurdles are made from thick hazel wands bent round stronger stakes. They are available as ready-made panels to fix to stakes hammered into the ground. Make your own in situ by weaving birch or other flexible prunings.*

4 The cut rail ends should reach to the centre line of the posts. Drill clearance holes into the rails to avoid splitting the wood close to the ends. Push the screws into the clearance holes and attach the first rail end to the centre of the post.

5 Offer up the next length of rail so that it is aligned with the end of the first one and sits up flush against it. Drill clearance holes as before, again taking care not to split the ends of the wood, and secure the rail to the post.

Apply a microporous paint or stain to the rails. Traditional paints and varnishes soon crack and peel off.

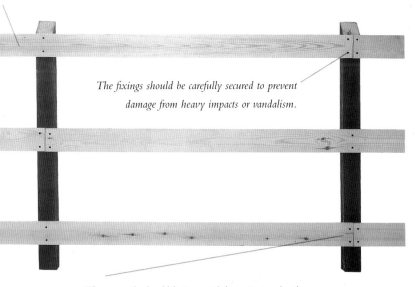

The fixings should be carefully secured to prevent damage from heavy impacts or vandalism.

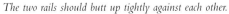

The two rails should butt up tightly against each other.

Erecting a pergola

Skill level:

DIY skills useful

Best time to do:

Anytime

Special tools required:

Striking block (can be hired), and mallet for driving in the staked post sockets

Time required:

May take the whole day or longer

WHAT YOU WILL NEED

• Flat packed self-assembly pergola complete with trellis panel infills
• Gloves
• Galvanized nails and a hammer
• Stepladder
• Metal sockets for securing posts to the ground
• Striking block (can be hired) and mallet for driving metal stake sockets into ground
• Microporous paint or stain

Self-assembly pergolas are available from garden centres and mail-order suppliers. Following the instructions, you should be able to put one together in just a few hours. The one featured on these pages has four uprights, two side beams, four cross beams and two trellis panels. But you can also buy the basic elements separately to construct a pergola of any proportion. The wood is treated with a preservative stain that will protect it from rotting and will not harm plants growing on it. When you have unpacked the kit and are ready to begin, it is a good idea to have someone to help you and you will also need a hammer, nails, gloves and a stepladder. Wear gloves to prevent splinters and as protection against the preservative stain applied to the wood. If you prefer to build a pergola from scratch, you can buy the wood from a timber merchant or builder's yard and either cut it yourself or ask them to cut and shape the various elements to your specification.

right: This large pergola, with its trellis walls covered in climbers, effectively creates an outdoor room, adding height to an otherwise rather flat landscape as well as a touch of style. Notice how the cross pieces and main posts are pleasingly substantial and the proportions give a spacious feel that allows for the growth of climbers. Making a pergola too low and narrow is a common mistake.

1 Support two of the uprights and lower one of the un-notched side beams into the groove. Decide on the spacing of these uprights before securing them into the ground. When you are happy with the overhang at each end of the side beam, secure it to the uprights with galvanised nails.

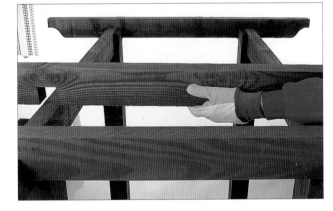

2 Once the two sides of the pergola are complete, join them together by dropping in one of the four cross beams. Put the end cross beams 'outside' the uprights for a more stable and generally stronger structure.

FIXING THE POSTS

Set the main posts into metal sockets driven into the ground or fixed in concrete to prevent them from rotting.

3 With the far end cross beam also in place, space the other two out equally. The width of the pergola is set by the notches in these cross beams. You may find that you need to tap them in gently with a hammer.

4 Nail the cross beams to the top of the side beams. Then position and nail the first trellis panel in between the uprights. Raise the panel 15cm(6in) off the ground to protect it from moisture and reduce the likelihood of rot.

Pots and Containers

You can grow pretty well anything in a pot provided it is large enough. In some circumstances, such as a tiny paved back yard or a roof garden, growing plants in containers is the only option. But generally speaking, the ability to garden in containers allows tremendous flexibility. You can put plants exactly where you want them – on walls, hung from pergolas, around the patio or driveway and in inhospitable areas such as ground with very thin, dry soil or root-filled ground under mature trees.

Containers can be grouped to create colourful displays that bring very different types of plants together – there really are no firm rules to be adhered to. What is more, with temporary plantings, you can ring the changes from season to season and year to year, experimenting with colour and form to your heart's content. You can even select plants to create a specific theme such as Oriental or Mediterranean.

Creative patio displays

Although you can grow plants in pots, window boxes and baskets anywhere in the garden, the patio, terrace or deck is likely to be where most of your containerised plants will be displayed. Some gardeners like to concentrate on seasonal colour, creating a bright and cheerful outlook from the house at the beginning of the year with bulbs. At the other extreme, there are permanent displays that utilise compact evergreens and deciduous flowering shrubs as well as perennials and groundcover plants. There is obviously a lot less work involved in the latter but the display is also likely to have less impact than one made exclusively with annuals, tender perennials and bulbs. A good compromise is to use elements from both types of display, using a framework of permanent plants,

right: *Drought-tolerant plants in simple clay pots make a stunning Mediterranean-style display on this hot, sunny patio.*

right: *You can be really inventive when it comes to containers. As long as something will hold soil and has enough room for the plants, the sky's the limit! Here an old metal water tank has been given a new lease of life and has been used to house a beautifully shaped Japanese maple; its rectangular shape makes a pleasing contrast and is a charming feature in a corner of the garden.*

Do:

• Group containers of different shapes and sizes to create more impact
• Use pots of the same colour or material to provide a linking theme
• Use baskets and wall pots to soften walls and vertical structures
• Use specific styles of container to emphasise a particular theme
• Include at least one large pot in a group of small containers to anchor the display

Don't:

• Only use seasonal flowers. Include some evergreen shrubs and trailers as framework planting within pot groupings
• Leave spent flowers or bulbs on show – use liners so that you can swap the pot with a fresh display
• Mix plants with different requirements in the same pot. Some will inevitably suffer and spoil the rest of the display

together with pots of seasonal colour that vary through the year. Once a pot is past its best, it can be removed from show and another substituted. To do this, put large containers on castors or moveable platforms or alternatively, to save moving heavy pots around, make use of liners. Simply plant up in ordinary plastic pots and drop these into their decorative covers, allowing room for fingers so that you can easily pull the pots out when you need to. If you forward plan and have substitutes waiting in the wings, there need never be any gaps. Create maximum impact with your displays by colour-coordinating the containers and their contents or by establishing a theme, for example a mix of terracotta pots and Mediterranean-style planting or glazed Chinese jars with Oriental-style plants and colour-scheming.

Planting bulbs for a spring display

With crocus, tulips and daffodils in containers, a patio can be a riot of colour from early spring onwards. There are two ways to use spring bulbs. The slow but cheap way is to plant dry bulbs in autumn using peat- or soil-based potting mixture. Choose compact varieties. Buy daffodils as soon as they are available and plant them straightaway, as they start rooting earlier than many spring bulbs. The bulbs should be plump and healthy, without cuts, bruises or mouldy bits; the biggest bulbs will bear the most flowers. You can plant containers entirely with one kind of bulb, but if you want to mix them, choose bulbs that flower at roughly the same time. After planting, stand portable containers outdoors in a cool, shady spot protected from heavy rain. When the first shoots appear, move them to the patio. Plant heavy tubs where they are to flower. While

A SPRING DISPLAY IN A PLASTIC CAULDRON

Inexpensive containers are ideal for brilliant spring displays; the secret is to pack them with plants. Spring bulbs and bedding plants just coming into bloom will not have time to make much more growth, so they must create immediate impact. Choose plants at roughly the same flowering stage.

1 Part-fill the container with potting mix and knock plants out of their pots. Avoid breaking up the rootballs or the plants may wilt and fade rapidly.

2 If the container will be seen from the front, plant the tallest flowers at the back with shorter kinds in front. This hides foliage and gives a fuller display.

3 Complete the display with a low spreading plant such as this winter-flowering heather at the front to soften the hard line created by the container rim. Leaving plants grouped together instead of splitting them up randomly throughout the display creates a stronger effect. Their foliage sets off each clump.

1 If your container does not have drainage holes in the base, drill some. Cover with crocks and add gravel.

2 Add 2.5-5cm(1-2in) of potting mix. In pots, it does not matter if bulbs are not planted with twice their own depth of potting mix.

3 Press each daffodil bulb gently down into the mix, giving it a half turn. This ensures that the base of the bulb makes good contact.

4 Cover the bulbs with enough mix to leave the tips on show so you can see where they are when you plant the next layer.

right: *This cross section shows the layers of bulbs in the container, with popular 'Golden Harvest' daffodils below and Anemone blanda 'Blue Shade' above.*

below: *Daffodils do best in the sun, but tolerate light shade. Anemone blanda grows to 15cm(6in) It is usually sold in mixed colours but single shades are sometimes available.*

5 Gently press in *Anemone blanda* corms between the tips of the lower layer of bulbs. Cover these corms with more mix.

6 Dot another layer of *Anemone blanda* over the surface, about 2.5cm(1in) above the last. Fill the tub to the rim with potting mix.

bulbs are flowering, feed them weekly with general-purpose liquid feed. When they are over, tip them out and plant them in the garden. Buy new bulbs for the following year's container displays, as they will flower better than the old ones.

For instant results, buy ready-grown spring bulbs in pots from the garden centre just as the buds are beginning to show colour.

Woodland-style tubs

Skill level:

Beginner gardener

Best time to do:

In spring, when the

plant is in bud or just

coming into flower

Special tools required:

None

Time required:

Less than an hour

WHAT YOU WILL NEED

• Dwarf or compact-growing
rhododendron
• Wooden barrel
• Plant-friendly wood
preservative
• Black plastic sheeting for lining
• Ericaceous and soil based
compost to mix
• Scissors
• Watering can or hose

Wooden half barrels are the favourite choice for permanently planting woodland shrubs, such as dwarf rhododendron, pieris or camellia, as they go so well together. You will need a large barrel, but do not choose one larger than you can comfortably move when it is full of soil. A 30cm(12in) container is the very smallest you should consider; 38-45cm(15-18in) is better and 60cm(24in) the ultimate. The larger the container, the larger the plant will be able to grow, as there will be more room for the roots. In a small pot the plant will be naturally dwarfed, but it will also dry out very quickly and need more frequent watering. To protect a wooden barrel from rot, paint it with a suitable preservative and line it with plastic as shown here.

The rhododendron featured here is a lime-hating plant that needs a lime-free potting mix and not the normal kind. Special lime-free (ericaceous) potting mixes are available, but these do not normally contain soil, being based on peat or coir instead. On their own, they are not ideal for plants that will be left in the same container for several years. You can make up your own mix, consisting of half ericaceous soil and half soil-based potting material. There is a little lime in this, but the mixture seems to suit ericaceous plants. Many heathers also need a lime-free potting mixture. Conifers and many other evergreen shrubs will be happy in this, too.

1 Allow the plastic sheet to hang over the sides of the barrel. This one is for a rhododendron, a lime-hating plant, so partly fill the barrel with a mixture of ericaceous and soil.

2 Knock the plant out of its pot and place it in the centre of the barrel. If the pot is filled with roots, gently tease a few of them out first, otherwise they will not be able to grow out into the mix.

3 Fill round the roots with more potting mix, leaving the top of the rootball level with the surface. The plant should be no deeper in the barrel than it was in the original pot.

4 Cut away the surplus plastic, leaving 5cm(2in) or so around the rim. This will be hidden.

5 Roll back the remaining plastic; tuck it inside the barrel edge to form a protective 'collar'.

PLANTING A SHADE BARREL

All kinds of evergreens make good specimen plants for shade. Camellias, pieris and rhododendrons do well in half barrels filled with ericaceous mix; replace the top layer of mix each spring and feed with a product containing sequestered iron to keep the plants healthy. Plants with striking leaves such as fatsia, the dramatic shapes of bamboo and the bright foliage colour of *Choisya ternata* 'Sundance' are all good subjects for tubs in shade. Or choose a piece of piece of clipped box topiary or a beautifully shaped Japanese maple.

Asplenium scolopendrium

Bergenia cordifolia 'Purpurea'

Gaultheria procumbens

6 Water the plant in well, so that the potting mix is thoroughly moist. Check it at least once a week and water again whenever the soil feels dry when you press a finger in it. One of the best large-flowered rhododendrons for growing in pots is *Rhododendron yakushimanum*.

above: *The contrasting foliage makes a great impact – the sword-shaped leaves of the hart's tongue fern set against the glossy, rounded bergenia foliage and fine-leaved gaultheria. The bergenia will flower in spring.*

Containers for winter colour

Skill level:

Beginner gardener

Best time to do:

Late autumn, when the

best selection of plants

for winter containers is

available

Special tools required:

None

Time required:

Between one and two

hours, once materials

have been assembled

WHAT YOU WILL NEED

• A range of winter interest
plants with a taller specimen to
act as a centrepiece
• Pot
• Matching pot 'feet' to allow
container to drain
• Crocks and gravel for drainage
(see previous page)
• Ericaceous compost

Festive holly and ivy foliage forms the basis of this winter container display, backed up by traditional berries and evergreen foliage, plus an ornamental cabbage, which makes a good alternative to winter flowers. If you cannot find a standard holly, you could remove all but one of the stems of an upright bush to convert it into an instant standard. Alternatively, use a columnar conifer such as a juniper. For a formal entrance, make a pair of matching pots and place one on either side of a porch. For a less formal look, team a single container with smaller but matching pots of evergreens, winter-flowering heathers and early spring bulbs. Keep winter displays in a well-sheltered spot, with containers raised up on pot feet and in as much light as possible. Even plants that normally prefer partial shade will thrive in better light during the dull winter days. To help insulate the roots of plants in smallish pots, stand each one inside a decorative container and pack the space between the two pots with bark chippings. Check containers regularly, even in winter, to see if they need watering; normal rainfall may not be able to get through dense foliage and into the potting mixture. Feed plants during mild spells in spring. Pick off discoloured leaves and generally tidy up container displays every week. If elements of winter bedding begin to look shabby, dig them out and drop in a replacement.

Skimmia japonica
'Rubella'

Cultivated
primrose
hybrids

Variegated
ivy

left: *For maximum impact with winter displays, make use of winter- and spring-flowering bedding such as hardy primrose hybrids, e.g. 'Husky' and 'Wanda' hybrids; Polyanthus 'Crescendo'; violas and pansies e.g. 'Universal' and 'Ultima' and double daisies (Bellis). Team these with evergreen shrubs and trailers with coloured or variegated foliage, berries and flowers, paying particular attention to colour-scheming. The skimmia used for the centre-piece of this tub gives excellent value.*

1 Assemble the plants and remove them from their pots before planting. Despite its name, 'Golden King', the standard holly, is a female that bears red berries provided it has been pollinated. Cover the drainage hole with a crock and part-fill the pot with an ericaceous potting mix, but leave enough room for the plant roots.

2 Stand the holly in the centre; add the golden tree heather at the base to soften the upright line of the trunk. Firm in gently.

3 Plant gaultheria and heather towards the front so that they overflow the edge. Tuck potting mix around their roots and firm in.

PLANTING UP A MIXED BARREL

A miniature garden in a barrel makes an easy-care, year-round display. Suitable subjects include dwarf conifers, heathers and grassy plants and even very compact shrubs, but check how big and how fast each plant grows so that the scheme does not become unbalanced.

4 Add a tall ornamental cabbage at the back. Plant the ivy, so that it curls round the sides of the pot for an instantly mature effect.

5 Fill any gaps with potting mix. Stand the display on pot feet, water it well and do not allow it to dry out. Do not feed until spring.

below: *Garden centres now sell an amazing range of plants for winter tubs and baskets, so a display like this is surprisingly easy to create.*

Ilex x altaclerensis 'Golden King'

Erica arborea 'Albert's Gold'

Ornamental cabbage

Calluna vulgaris 'Alexandra'

Gaultheria procumbens

Hedera helix 'Sagittifolia' has long, narrow, arrowhead-shaped leaves.

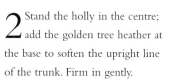

Planting a patio rose

Skill level:

Beginner gardener

Best time to do:

Preferably late spring,

when you can view the

new rose plants in the

garden centres

Special tools required:

None

Time required:

Less than an hour

Although climbing and rambler roses can be grown on the patio, up walls and over pergola poles, they must be planted in the ground, in beds of good, deep soil. They will not do well in containers, even large ones, for very long. Only two kinds of roses are really suitable for growing in tubs, namely patio roses and miniature roses. Patio roses are like compact versions of the larger floribundas and hybrid teas, growing to 45-60cm(18-24in) high. Miniature roses are really small – growing to 23-45cm(9-18in) high, according to variety, with densely clustered stems. Choose a well-shaped plant with evenly spaced branches, healthy foliage and plenty of flowerbuds. Use a large container and a good-quality, soil-based potting mixture. It is vital to keep potted roses very well fed and watered, as they are growing in a very limited volume of soil. Daily watering may be needed in summer, even if the pot is a large one. Feed every week from the time growth starts in spring until late summer, using liquid rose feed. Top dress in spring with pelleted or seaweed manure. Prune patio roses as you would normal bush roses in early spring. Miniature roses do not really need any pruning apart from a light tidy-up in late spring to remove dead twigs. They are not quite as hardy as other types of rose and rather prone to frost damage so move pots to a sheltered spot or inside an unheated greenhouse from early winter. Combine potted roses with other plants or use as specimens.

WHAT YOU WILL NEED

• A patio rose chosen for disease resistance
• A plastic-lined clay pot with matching saucer or a glazed pot
• Crocks and gravel for drainage
• Good-quality soil-based potting mix
• A trowel

1 Choose a pot in proportion to the size of the rose. You can use a clay or plastic pot, but clay looks better. Cover the base of the pot with good-quality, soil-based potting mix.

2 Tip the plant out of its pot. If it does not slide out easily, turn the pot on its side and knock the rim gently against something solid. Support the rootball gently with your fingers to stop it falling apart.

3 Stand the plant in the middle of the pot, teasing out any large roots. Fill the gap around the edge of the rootball with a little more potting mixture.

4 Firm the soil down gently, leaving a 2.5cm(1in) gap between the top of the soil and the rim of the pot to allow for watering. Water thoroughly.

A CHERRY TREE FOR THE PATIO

A fruit garden takes up valuable space in a small plot; if this is a problem, then growing in pots may be a solution. Many tree fruits, particularly those grown on dwarfing rootstocks make good patio pot subjects as they have pretty spring blossom as well as attractive fruits. Peaches and cherries are best grown as dwarf trees or as fan-trained plants – a handy way of growing them against a wall where it is easier to protect the ripening fruit from birds.

The cherry below is planted in a large plastic-lined terracotta pot, big enough to accommodate the root ball with a frame of bamboo canes.

right: *Cherry trees on dwarfing rootstock are available ready-trained from larger garden centres and specialist fruit nurseries. The variety shown here is 'Morello', an acid cherry used for cooking. Its fruits are ready to pick in midsummer.*

5 Stand the pot on a matching saucer, which should be in proportion to the size of the pot. Remove this for improved winter drainage.

left: *Miniature roses have dainty flowers and make excellent subjects for containers on the patio where they can be appreciated at close quarters.*

Tie the new shoot growth to the bamboo frame and check older ties are not too tight

As necessary, re-attach branches to a larger frame

Seek advice on correct pruning and training

Flowers in wicker baskets

Skill level:

Beginner gardener

Best time to do:

Late spring to

midsummer, when

potted herbaceous are

available in garden

centres

Special tools required:

None

Time required:

Less than an hour

WHAT YOU WILL NEED

• Range of colour-coordinated herbaceous perennials
• A wicker basket
• Yacht varnish or coloured stain to pre-treat the basket
• Black plastic sheeting
• Gravel for drainage
• Potting mix
• Scissors
• Bark mulch
• Bricks or wooden chocks to stand the basket on

In summer, old and new wicker baskets make superb temporary plant containers, either to conceal plastic pots or to create an instant display. Treat them first with two coats of yacht varnish or apply a coloured stain and allow it to dry thoroughly. If you intend to plant directly into a basket, line it with black plastic before filling it with potting mix to protect the wicker from discoloring or rotting. Natural baskets look particularly good filled with exuberant country garden flowers. For a tall upright basket, choose plants that are one-and-a-half times to twice its height to maintain the correct proportions. In a wide shallow trug, a low display of trailing annuals would look good; add a climber to grow up over the handle. In shade, try alternate green and gold varieties of *Soleirolia soleirolii* or fill generously with *Duchesnea indica* (false strawberry) for an artistic 'still-life' effect. In the garden, always stand a basket up on bricks to permit the air to circulate underneath and prevent rotting. Do not leave baskets outdoors in winter, as they quickly deteriorate in bad weather, even when protected by varnish. Wicker baskets are perfectly at home in country or cottage garden settings but also look good in contemporary gardens with an informal feel, especially in conjunction with wood and other natural materials.

1 Loosely line a wicker basket with black plastic and make a few holes in the bottom. Place 5cm (2in) of clean gravel into the base.

2 Part-fill the basket with good-quality potting mixture. Leave the top of the plastic liner rolled over the top of the basket for now.

3 Put the tallest plants – here lythrum – at the centre-back of the display in order to create a graduated effect. This allows all the plants to be seen properly. Use a mix of flower shapes; contrast spires of astilbe with the chunkier, flat-topped shapes of verbena. Contrast is important in displays that use mainly colour.

4 Top up with potting mixture, then roll the liner over to make a firm edge and tuck it just inside the rim of the basket.

5 A chipped bark mulch looks decorative, teams well with the natural cane basket and helps to keep plant roots cool and moist.

Lythrum salicaria 'Blush'

Achillea millefolium rosea

Penstemon 'Andenken an Friedrich Hahn'

Phygelius 'Winchester Fanfare'

Astilbe arendsii hybrid

6 If the finished basket is too awkward or heavy to move easily and you do not have help, use a small wheeled trolley or even a skateboard to manoeuvre it into its final position.

VARIATIONS ON THE THEME Still keeping with the cottage or country garden theme, this wicker basket is planted with a mixture of herbs and flowers including parsley, chives, stocks and lobelia. Some annuals look more like wildflowers and are great for baskets. Try cornflowers, calendula or foxgloves.

The terracotta terrace

Skill level:

Beginner gardener

Best time to do:

From late spring to

midsummer. Keep the

arrangement frost-free

and on the dry side

over winter

Special tools required:

None

Time required:

Less than an hour

WHAT YOU WILL NEED

• Selection of succulents to give varied texture and colour – you may have to look in the houseplant and alpine sections of your garden centre
• Terracotta trough – there is no need to line with polythene
• Gravel for added drainage
• A gritty potting mix suitable for alpines

Most garden centres sell a wonderful range of terracotta containers. Some are very simple clay pots whilst others are highly ornate. The colour can vary too, ranging from almost powdery white to deep, smoky-brown. This is partly to do with the way the clay is fired. Always check whether the pots are merely frost resistant or frost proof.

A collection of simple terracotta pots and jars on the terrace evokes a feeling of hot sunny climes – somewhere in the Mediterranean perhaps! This impression is amplified by using certain kinds of plants – spiky specimens, those with succulent leaves or hot coloured flowers, and so on. Ornamental grasses, sedges and various grass-like plants are all the rage now, since gardeners have begun to realise the potential of these wonderful plants. Tufted grasses like the deschampsias, and ones with blue foliage – for example *Helictotrichon sempervirens* and *Festuca glauca* – look great in terracotta.

below: A variegated phormium takes centre stage in a large terracotta pot with grasses and sedges slotted into purpose-built planting areas within the decking.

SUCCULENTS IN PLAIN TERRACOTTA

Try experimenting with different combinations of succulents. The large rounded echeverias in this display came from the houseplant section of a garden centre, but like most succulents, they prefer to be outdoors for the summer.

Sedum spurium 'Purple Carpet'

Echeveria hybrid

3 Finally add one or two pots of variegated *Sedum lineare*. This grows more quickly; pinch it out regularly.

Sedum lineare 'Variegatum'

1 Position the purple-leaved sedum in one corner so the foliage drapes over the side. Plant the blue-grey echeveria.

2 Tuck the silvery sedum under the echeveria where it can fill out gradually. Add the second echeveria, again at the front.

Sedum spathulifolium 'Cape Blanco'

Echeveria hybrid

PLANTING A NARROW-NECKED JAR

To avoid filling the whole jar with potting mix, wedge a hanging basket snugly into the neck of the pot, plant with ivies and simply lodge it in position. It can be easily and safely lifted out when the plants need to be replaced or given fresh potting mixture.

Evergreen trailers, such as ivy, accentuate the shape of the jar without competing for attention.

left: *These three different grass specimens planted into simple terracotta pots and set against a backdrop of bamboo, make a simple but dramatic statement.*

A classic urn for autumn

Plastic containers are probably the cheapest you can buy, yet with care they can be made to look much more expensive. Choose a classic formal shape, such as an urn, cornucopia, or bowl. If the container is to go on a pedestal later, choose one that is correctly proportioned for its base. Use paint effects to create a fake stone or verdigris finish, but do this long before you intend planting the container, as it takes several coats to achieve the desired result and thorough drying between coats is essential. Give the shiny surface of a plastic container a rough finish before painting, using sandpaper.

1 This plastic urn was offered at half price as a shop-soiled item. Scrubbing it with soapy water cleans off the grime and prepares it for painting.

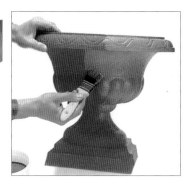

2 To build up the look of aged stone or verdigris, you will need three subtle shades of water-based matt emulsion paint or artist's acrylics.

3 When the red oxide primer is dry, apply the first layer of emulsion paint. This drab grey-brown shade acts as as an excellent solid background to the paler tones.

WHAT YOU WILL NEED

- Plastic urn
- Sandpaper
- Water-based matt emulsion paints or artist's acrylics
- Paintbrushes, short-bristled stencil brush
- Clear matt acrylic varnish
- Selection of plants, plus gravel, crocks and compost to plant up when paint has thoroughly dried

4 Use a short-bristled stencil brush to dab the dusky green paint onto the urn when the drab coat is dry. Press the brush against the urn in short, sharp dabs.

5 To take the transformation a stage further, wait for the green paint to dry and then use the stencil brush to dab on some of the pale blue-green emulsion paint.

6 To protect the paint from the weather, apply a coat or two of acrylic varnish. It is milky as you put it, on but it dries clear and will enhance the paint finish as well.

Gaultheria mucronata

Sedum spectabile

Winter-flowering heather

Variegated ivies

Ornamental cabbage

1 Place 2.5cm(1in) of washed gravel or crocks into the urn for drainage. It already has small holes to allow water to run out. Fill the urn to within 5cm(2in) of the rim with good-quality potting mixture. Leave the mixture loose and fluffy for planting.

2 Begin planting from the back, starting with the tallest plants. Choose those that tone well together in colour, but provide varied shapes and textures for added interest and impact. This is only a temporary display, so feel free to use a mixture of whatever plants look good together and are the right size.

3 Bold ornamental cabbages provide solid colour that makes a good focal point to the display. Lean them over at an angle (even over the side of the urn) so that they make the most impact. Finish off by tucking a few trailing ivies around the front of the urn, to soften the edge and help frame the focal point.

4 Combining the ornamental cabbage with flowers, berries, and foliage produces a varied end result that will remain attractive for a long period.

COMPOSING THE PICTURE

When selecting plants, do not just pick those with flowers of a colour that will coordinate with their container; aim for a mixture of strong shapes that work well together, so that each flower stands out from its background.

Wall containers with character faces

Skill level:

Beginner gardener

Best time to do:

Anytime of year using

hardened-off plants

Special tools required:

Electric drill to make

holes for drainage and

wall fixings

Time required:

Less than an hour

A wall pot with a carved face adds a theatrical touch to the garden. The ancient craggy features and untamed beard of the male character certainly look well with the wild 'locks' of trailing ivy and bring to mind the Green Man legend. By contrast the mysterious female character seems to suit the somewhat softer planting of daisies and delicate silver foliage. Create more realistic 'hair' in all kinds of head planters – modern or classical, using evergreen grasses and grass-like plants such as *Carex* 'Snowline' and 'Evergold', blue-leaved festucas or the black-leaved *Ophiopogon planiscapus* 'Nigrescens'. Whatever you use, keep planting as simple as possible to highlight the features rather than competing with them. And double the dramatic effect by placing his 'n' hers wall masks either side of a doorway.

1 Once the paint effect has dried, drill holes in the base of the plastic pot, then add a couple of inches of gravel for drainage.

2 Cover the gravel with potting mixture, filling the wall pot but allowing space on top for the ivies. Try one of the plants for size.

3 Squeeze the rootballs into ovals so that you can plant as many different kinds of ivy in the top as possible to make a thick head of hair.

WHAT YOU WILL NEED

• A plastic, head-shaped wall planter (ready painted) or terracotta planter
• Gravel
• Electric drill to make drainage holes
• Trowel
• Potting mixture
• Selection of plain green and variegated ivy (the less variegation the hardier the plant)

4 Fill the gaps between the plants with more potting mix, and water the plants. Hang the pot on the wall in a sheltered, shady position to prevent damage by cold winds or scorching in strong sun.

1 Mix a small amount of white, yellow and dark green acrylic paint with water until the mixture becomes quite runny. Tilt the pot and apply the first coat.

2 If the terracotta colour does not start to show through soon, use a clean, wet brush and go over the raised portions of the face again, diluting the paint.

3 Using a pad of damp kitchen towel, dab off some of the paint from the raised parts of the face in irregular patches.

4 Once dry, apply a second coat. The paint runs down in streaks, much like weathering caused by damp conditions.

5 When dry, mix up some dark green paint and water. Using a damp, natural sponge, dab over the surface and work paint into the crevices of the face.

FAKE TERRACOTTA

Plastic 'terracotta' can be reasonably convincing but it doesn't weather and continues to look quite 'raw'. Use paint effects to mimic natural weathering.

Paint pigments separate out, adding to the illusion of age.

right: *Once fixed onto the wall, no one would realise that this was in fact a plastic pot; it looks so much like an old, algae-covered terracotta planter.*

Real terracotta will weather in time but you can 'age' it too.

Hanging gardens

Hanging baskets, wall pots and window boxes allow you to cultivate what is to all intents and purposes a hostile environment – the wall of a house is like a sheer cliff face with no toeholds! But fix in a few screws, hooks and brackets and you can transform bare bricks into luxuriant hanging gardens.

Generally speaking, the display is only temporary, so you can ring the changes from season to season and have great fun experimenting with different plants and colour schemes. Break some gardening rules and mix alpines with bedding plants, houseplants with herbs and shrubs with tender

above: *Brightly-coloured annuals including geraniums and tuberous begonias form this exuberant window box display. Pick plants that will emphasise the style or character already established in your garden.*

right: *Matching baskets hung at equal heights effectively screen the area underneath the pergola from view. This formal arrangement has far more impact than if the baskets were all differently planted.*

perennials! Once you branch out, the palette of colours and textures available to you increases enormously. Baskets and wall containers are available in a wide range of materials and designs and though they are mainly a feature of the summer garden, this certainly does not have to be the case. Even in the depths of winter, you can enjoy wonderful displays of fresh flowers, colourful berries and foliage around the doors and windows.

No matter how tiny a backyard you have, there will always be space for hanging baskets. Even if the ground is paved, bare walls and fences can be instantly transformed into a hanging garden. In a

Do:

• Colour scheme your arrangements for greater impact
• Use plenty of drought tolerant plants in case of missed waterings
• Experiment with different 'ingredients', ensuring that plants purchased from the under cover area of the nursery or garden centre have been properly hardened off first
• Use liners in window boxes

Don't:

• Forget to water and feed regularly. If this is difficult, use self-watering containers with an internal reservoir or install automatic irrigation
• Hang baskets where the trails will get in the way of human traffic or where drips will cause problems.
• Underestimate the amount of 'preening' needed to maintain an attractive display
• Use inappropriate fixings for baskets and window boxes

right: *The Surfinia petunias revolutionised the world of hanging baskets with their vigourous and floriferous nature. They are now available in many different colours, but the most striking displays come from planting just one variety. This can be a risky strategy in a basket because if a particular kind of plant does not perform well one year, the whole display suffers. Use a reliable performer like the so-called balcony geraniums.*

new plot, where climbers and wall shrubs are still very small, trailing foliage can cover the gaps easily and provide a continuation of colour from the border up. Baskets and wall containers can also be used to draw the eye towards an attractive feature, such as a house nameplate or decorative window, and there are a number of ways to make such vertical displays even more eye-catching. Hang an identical basket on either side of a doorway and straight away you have doubled the effect. And, with several baskets hanging in a line, it is possible to create a continuous ribbon of colour. This technique is all the more effective if the plants are chosen to fit into a particular colour scheme.

How to hang a basket

Skill level:

Beginner gardener;

some DIY experience

useful

Best time to do:

Hang baskets when all

risk of frost has passed

and during mild spells

Special tools required:

Electric hammer-action

drill

Time required:

A couple of hours

WHAT YOU WILL NEED

• Self-watering hanging basket
• Potting mix suitable for baskets
• Range of plants including
trailers – select for a spring,
summer, autumn or winter
display
• Trowel
• Wall bracket (check size correct
for diameter of basket)
• Electric, hammer-action drill,
wall plugs, screwdriver

Hanging baskets are traditionally suspended by a doorway, a little above head height, where the shape and style of the display can be best appreciated. However, there are plenty of other options. Hang them from the end of pergola poles, from special, free-standing hanging basket support frames – which take several baskets at different heights – or suspend a collection of baskets from brackets to decorate a large plain wall. Wall planters are more often used in the latter situation, but being smaller they are better suited to more intimate spots, where they add fine detail.

below: *This stunning basket of mixed hybrid clematis has been hung from the bough of a tree and illustrates the potential for inventive basket displays.*

A SELF-WATERING BASKET

If regular watering presents problems, then a self-watering hanging basket is the perfect solution.
Immediately after planting, water the basket in the normal way to ensure that the potting mixture
is thoroughly wetted. Thereafter, water will be drawn up from the reservoir at the bottom of the
basket, as and when the plants require it. Use the tube to fill the reservoir and avoid overwatering.

Primula denticulata 'Alba'   *Primula* (hardy hybrid primrose)

Euonymus japonicus 'Aureus'   *Variegated ivy*

1 Feed the wick through the base plate. It draws water up from the reservoir and keeps the capillary matting damp.

2 Push the watering tube through the hole in the base plate before adding potting mix. You will be able to camouflage it easily.

3 Completely cover the capillary matting with a layer of moist potting mix formulated for hanging baskets. Plant up the basket.

4 Hang the basket in a lightly shaded, sheltered spot and water it via the tube. Remove individual blooms as they fade.

1 Put the bracket against the wall and mark the position of the screw holes. Using a hammer-action drill and the correct sized masonry bit, drill the top hole in the wall. Push a wall plug into the hole, making sure that it fits tightly. It will prevent the screw working loose.

2 Fix the top screw loosely so that you can check the position of the second hole. Make any necessary adjustments.

3 Drill and plug the second hole and screw the bracket firmly in place against the wall. Use matching round-headed screws.

right: *Choose the correct size of bracket. Too big a basket and it will buckle under the weight. Allow room for the basket to grow but still be clear of the wall.*

Easy step-by-steps to a traditional basket

Skill level:

Some experience with

handling delicate plants

useful

Best time to do:

Plant in early summer

after the risk of frost

has passed

Special tools required:

None

Time required:

A couple of hours

WHAT YOU WILL NEED

• Wire basket (35–40cm/14–16in) with wide gaps to allow for planting through the sides
• Sphagnum moss
• Circle of plastic, e.g. cut from an old potting mix bag
• Potting mix suitable for baskets
• Range of summer flowering plants and foliage chosen to give maximum contrast in form and texture

There are all kinds of hanging basket liners, but none so attractive as living sphagnum moss. Being soft, green and moisture-retentive, it allows for plants to be tucked in through the sides of the basket, plugging any gaps in an attractive way. This is the traditional technique and is not as hard as it looks – you just need patience! It is a good idea to soak the moss in a bucket of water before you begin, just to make sure it has absorbed its full capacity, then lightly squeeze the excess before use. The secret to success with moss is not to skimp on it, otherwise the potting mix will leak and the vulnerable rootballs will tend to dry out.

Obviously, the smaller the rootball of the plant, the easier it is to manipulate it through the wires of the hanging basket, but you can squeeze larger rootballs into an oval to fit them through more easily. Alternatively, use a piece of stiff paper to roll the shoots up so that the plant can be fed from the inside of the basket out. With pots of bedding ivy, simply split the compost apart with your fingers and plant the rooted cuttings individually.

VARIATIONS ON THE THEME

When making up baskets for spring display, you have two choices – either you plan ahead in autumn and plant dry bulbs within the arrangement, or you make an instant display, buying plants already in flower in spring, including potted bulbs.

right: *This fresh, vibrant basket features a pleasing mix of spring flowers and bulbs and is set off perfectly by the traditional basket lining of sphagnum moss.*

1 Stand the basket on a bucket for stability. Cut a circle from an old potting mix bag and place it black side down in the basket. Fill the plastic circle with potting mix.

2 The plastic acts as a reservoir for the plants, trapping water and preventing soil from washing through. Tuck sphagnum moss under the edges for camouflage.

3 Cover the basket sides with the sweetly scented white alyssum, feeding the rootballs through the gaps so that they rest horizontally on the soil.

4 Pack moss around the necks of the plants to stop them drying out. Add a busy Lizzie, a pot of *Lotus berthelotii*, white petunias, ivy, and a white pelargonium.

5 Fill in any remaining gaps with soil and cover the surface with a thick mulch of moist sphagnum moss. Water the basket copiously using a fine rose to settle the soil in around the plants. Replace the chains and hang in a sunny, sheltered spot.

Pelargonium *PAC cultivar* 'Aphrodite' (zonal pelargonium)

Petunia 'Celebrity White'

Impatiens *F1 hybrid* (busy Lizzie)

Lotus berthelotii (parrot's beak)

Hedera helix (variegated ivy)

CLASSIC WHITE This combination of white, grey, silver and green is classically elegant. But monochrome schemes only work with plenty of textural contrast. Here the large, solid flower heads of petunia are planted against the smaller-flowered busy Lizzie, which in turn is set against a froth of white alyssum. Foliage is equally important – ferny, grey-leaved lotus against trailing ivy, both contrasting well with the rounded geranium leaves. There are pure whites and creamy whites – don't mix them, but do drop in touches of lavender-blue, salmon pink or lime to enhance the whiteness of the flowers.

Lobularia maritima 'Snow Crystals' (sweet white alyssum)

A summer basket using rooted cuttings

Skill level:

Some experience of

raising plants under

glass useful

Best time to do:

Early to mid-spring

Special tools required:

None

Time required:

Once all the

'ingredients' are

assembled, allow one

to two hours

WHAT YOU WILL NEED

• A range of plugs, net pots or young plants from the garden centre or your own seedlings and rooted cuttings
• Wire hanging basket
• Sphagnum moss
• Circle of black plastic
• Pair of scissors
• Potting mix

Most people plant up hanging baskets in early summer, using good-sized plants that are already in full bloom to make an immediate display. Since all risk of frost is past by then, the containers can safely be put straight out into the garden. But if you have space in a heated greenhouse or conservatory, you can plant the containers much earlier and grow them on under cover. This is a good way to use home-grown seedlings of bedding plants, or rooted cuttings of fuchsias and pelargoniums. However, you can also take advantage of the wide range of 'plug' plants, and 'tots' in net pots or small plastic pots available from early spring. Later in the season small plants will be harder to find. 'Plugs' are young plants grown in small individual 'cells', rather like multiple egg boxes on a tiny scale. Remove each plantlet from its cell before planting, by pushing the tip of a dibber or pencil carefully up through the base of the cell. Alternatively, stab a tiny fork into the potting mixture to lift out the plantlet. Plugs make planting very simple; root damage is virtually non-existent, as the plugs can simply be pushed into loose potting mix. They are particularly easy to use around the sides of hanging baskets, as they are small enough to fit through the wire sides of traditional baskets.

1 Assemble a mixture of flowering and foliage plants, with trailing varieties to cover the basket sides and bushy, upright types for the middle.

2 Place a circle of black plastic in the bottom of the basket to act as a water reservoir. Add some potting mixture to hold it in place.

Net pots should be left in place during planting, but you must remove solid pots.

3 Tuck a layer of sphagnum moss under the edge of the plastic. Once the basket is full, you will not notice the plastic at all.

4 Build up the sides with a thick layer of moss. Pack it in tightly to prevent soil escaping when the plants are watered. Add more mix.

5 Gently push the neck of the plant just inside the wire. Pack it with moss and cover the rootball with more mix. Plant the ivy, holding the root-ball horizontally and feeding the trails through the wires from the inside out. Push the crown against the inside of the basket.

6 When the sides are planted up, cover all the exposed rootballs with more mix. Leave space for planting in the top. Add more trailing plants to hang over the top of the basket. Fill in the centre with upright plants; leave room for plant growth.

7 Cover the surface with a thick layer of moss, Water the basket well and hang it in a light, frost-free place until the plants are established. Once young plants develop a good root system, they quickly fill the basket. Feed regularly to keep them flowering.

BEST CULTIVARS

SINGLES: Abigail, Aunty Jinks, Daisy Bell, Hermiena, Jack Shahan, Marinka, President Margaret Slater, Red Spider, Waveney Gem

DOUBLES: Applause, Blush O' Dawn, Dancing Flame, Devonshire Dumpling, Frau Hilde Rademacher, Malibu Mist, Pink Galore, Pink Marshmallow, Seventh Heaven, Swingtime, Wilson's Pearls

below: *This is Lucinda, a semi-double fuchsia that will flower profusely throughout the summer.*

left: *Single-flowered fuchsias are delightfully simple; most have four petals. They create elegant displays.*

Verbena 'Blue Cascade'

Fuchsia 'Beacon' (bush variety)

Hedera helix (variegated ivy)

Fuchsia 'La Campanella' (cascade variety)

Glechoma hederacea 'Variegata'

Brachyscome multifida

A fuchsia flower tower

Skill level:

Some experience with

planting hanging

baskets an advantage

Best time to do:

Early spring with rooted

cuttings to late spring

and early summer with

larger plants

Special tools required:

None

Time required:

Allow up to two hours

WHAT YOU WILL NEED

• Sufficient young plantlets to fill the tower once they have grown. Use only one variety or a good mixture, e.g. an F1 hybrid mix of impatiens
• Flower tower
• Potting mix suitable for hanging baskets
• Trowel
• Scissors

Today, the choice of containers for hanging displays is wider than ever. A recent development is a design based on a sturdy plastic bag. Follow the instructions for assembling a container like this; the one shown here has an integral drip tray that prevents splashing and also acts as a small extra water reservoir. Since the aim is to cover the sides as quickly as possible, choose fast-growing trailing plants with a dense branching habit and do not economise on the number of plants you buy. Trailing fuchsias and petunias are good, but also consider solenopsis, bidens, and Swiss balcon pelargoniums. There is no need to buy large plants. Small 'plug' plants (see page 174) are ideal, since their tiny, narrow, rootballs are easy to push in through slits or crosses cut in the sides of the bag. If only larger plants are available, remove loose mix from the rootball and tease out the roots to give a longer narrower shape that is easier to get into the bag.

above: *Trailing verbena makes a more traditional display. The dusky pink flowers contrast particularly well with the delicate ferny foliage. Look for plants with similar attributes for alternative schemes.*

above: *Oxalis makes an unusual subject for this tower, but all sorts of plants with plenty of small bright flowers and contrasting dark foliage, especially if strikingly shaped, would work, too.*

ALTERNATIVE PLANTING SCHEMES The same sort of containers can be used for all kinds of bedding plant schemes; different types can be mixed together in much the same way as you might plant a hanging basket, but for most dramatic displays use all the same type of plant, or even all the same variety.

1 This hanging 'tower' has plastic sides and a solid drip tray base. Assemble and suspend it and add a layer of potting mix.

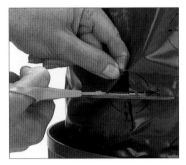

2 Cut four or five crosses just above the level of the potting mixture in the base, where you want to put plants. Prepare and plant only one layer at a time.

3 Tip small trailing fuchsias out of their pots, remove surplus soil from the roots and squeeze them gently into a narrow column that will fit through the crosses.

4 Gently tuck the roots inside the bag so that they rest on the surface of the potting mix. Tuck the plastic back around the neck of the plant to stop the mix falling out.

5 With the bottom row of plants in place, add another layer of mix. Do this slowly and evenly so that the wrinkles in the sides of the container are stretched out. Cut more crosses halfway up the side walls, staggering them.

6 Put in a final row of plants as close as possible to the top of the container. Finish with a large single plant, which could be of a more upright type than the others. Water evenly, so that the mix is moistened but is not washed out.

Nip out the tips of any shoots that spoil the shape of the display.

Baskets for winter colour

From autumn to early winter, garden centres stock all the ingredients you need to make up some imaginative baskets. Many young shrubs in small pots are available at this time; they may seem quite expensive for a seasonal basket, but you can of course plant them out in the garden once the display is over. Pots of ivy with long trails are to be found in the houseplant section of garden centres; outdoor ones are rarely so luxuriant. Gradually introduce the ivy to outdoor conditions and temperatures before planting it. Although more often associated with summer bedding displays, some plants, such as *Senecio cineraria*, are reasonably hardy and it is worth potting up a few plants towards the end of summer. Cut back long straggly shoots or flower stems to promote bushy new growth and keep them in a sunny spot for use later on. Conifer hedge clippings make a good substitute for moss in baskets. Their fresh green colouring is very welcome in winter and lasts for months without turning brown.

1 Cut a circle of plastic from an old potting mixture bag and use it black-side-down to line the base of a wire basket.

2 Add some potting mixture to act as a small reservoir that helps to prevent water from draining away too rapidly.

3 Build up the conifer lining, tucking the foliage under the edge of the plastic circle. Weave the pieces into each other.

WHAT YOU WILL NEED

• Conifer clippings
• Range of foliage and flowering plants for winter colour including an ivy with long trails
• Circle of black plastic
• Potting mix
• Trowel
• Wire basket

VARIATIONS ON THE THEME As an alternative to hardy primroses and heathers, try winter-flowering pansies, for example 'Universal' and 'Ultima' F1 hybrid series. These perform especially well but you will find lots of other varieties in late autumn, including the subtle 'Antique Shades' and small-flowered violas. Buy trays with at least one or two flowers open. Hang pansy baskets under cover during very cold spells

4 Add more potting mix until you reach the point where the first plant is to go in. Offer up the euonymus and adjust the soil level.

5 Continue to build up the conifer lining, adding more potting mix. Plant the silver cineraria followed by the primroses.

PLANTING UP A HEATHER BASKET

With their compact shape and free-flowering habit, winter-flowering heathers are ideal for hanging baskets. Buy evenly shaped plants just coming into flower at the start of the season and fill up the basket, as plants cannot be expected to grow and hide gaps at that time of year.

Euonymus fortunei 'Emerald 'n' Gold'

Hybrid primroses

Senecio cineraria 'Silver Dust'

1 Half-fill the basket loosely with potting mix. Knock the ivy out of its pot and plant in the centre. Leave the long ivy trails tied to the cane. Add a couple of gold foliage heathers.

2 Fill the sides of the basket with flowering heathers so that the shoots cascade over the edges without swamping the gold-leaved heathers. Release the ivy trails from their support.

3 Arrange the ivy trails to cascade over the edge of the basket and through the heathers. Also train some around the chains. Hang fairly low so that you can see inside.

Hedera helix 'Ester'

6 Add another euonymus and a trailing ivy, water in well and allow to drain. Water again when the surface of the potting mix starts to dry out.

Wire wall baskets and hay racks

Skill level:

Some experience of

planting baskets useful

Best time to do:

Early summer

Special tools required:

None

Time required:

Up to an hour, not

including fixing the

supports for the basket

or hay rack

WHAT YOU WILL NEED

• Geraniums and variegated
Felicia amelloides
• Wirework basket
• Black polythene for lining
• Sphagnum moss
• Potting mix
• Heavy screws to act as hooks
on which to hang the basket on
the wall

From early spring, garden centres are stocked with potted bulbs and spring bedding - perfect for a splash of instant colour. These are followed by a myriad of summer bedding varieties, including annuals and tender perennials. Certain fruit and vegetables also do well in baskets, so try mixing in cascading tomatoes or strawberries. And do not forget scent and aroma. Among the herbs, you will find many varieties with colourful foliage. For summer baskets a plant's ability to survive heat and drought is of prime importance and the pelargonium comes close to being the perfect candidate. Available in a wide range of vibrant shades, pelargoniums could be used in a basket all by themselves. In the simple arrangement (right) they are teamed with felicia, another excellent drought-resistant plant.

Polyanthus 'Crescendo Primrose'

Tulipa 'The First'

Bellis perennis (double daisy)

VARIATION: A SPRING WALL BASKET A large, manger-style basket or hay rack can create an impressive wall feature. In this sparkling spring display, the polyanthus are the exact colour of wild primroses and to take the wild theme a step further, the spaces between all the plants are filled with moss, giving the impression of a bank in the hedgerow filled with spring flowers. There are several other colourways that work well. For example, if you want a more vivid scheme, try scarlet red tulips, white daisies, deep blue polyanthus and blue-and-white violas.

1 Line the back and base of the basket with plastic to prevent damp seeping into the wall behind. Trim off any excess at the top.

2 Firm down the moss. Add potting mix up to the point where you intend to plant through the front of the basket.

3 Rest the rootballs of the kingfisher daisies horizontally on the potting mix at varying heights. Tuck more moss around the plants.

4 Add the first of the ivy-leaved trailing pelargoniums, arranging the trailing stems so that they point out to the side.

5 Fill in any gaps with potting mix, and water the arrangement well. Hang it up by hooking the frame over two screws fixed into a sunny wall. Deadhead fading blooms.

Pelargonium 'Barock' (ivy-leaved geranium)

Felicia amelloides variegated

PLANTING A WINTER WALL BASKET

The festive looking winter cherry, available in autumn, makes an ideal subject for a sheltered wall basket by the front door during the holidays. Pure white mini-cyclamen can also be found at this time and though normally sold as houseplants, both may be hardened off.

Cyclamen persicum

Solanum pseudocapsicum 'Thurino'

Hedera helix 'Adam'

Hedera helix 'Hvid Kolibri'

Colour co-ordinating terracotta

Skill level:

Beginner gardener

Best time to do:

Early summer

Special tools required:

None

Time required:

Allow up to an hour

Painting terracotta may seem rather unconventional, but an effect like this is very easy to achieve. As an alternative colourway, try a mint-green base coat sponged over lightly with white to give a mottled effect and fill the windowbox with soft apricot tuberous begonias, fuchsias and busy Lizzies in shades of pink, peach and white, all with a foil of white-variegated foliage. A rich powder-blue would suit the strong orange and lemon shades found in a pot marigold mix such as *Calendula* 'Fiesta Gitana', or mixed nasturtiums such as 'Alaska'. Alternatively, use a mid purple-blue as a base coat and add touches of crimson, blue and white paint diluted with water to the relief pattern. Plant with deep purple, velvet red and light lavender-blue flowers and silver foliage. For example, at the back you might use *Salvia farinacea* 'Victoria' and in the foreground crimson-red verbena

and deep purple petunia, interplanted with silver cut-leaved cineraria and red trailing lobelia. Highly ornate terracotta windowboxes are perfect for a period setting, but if you plant with modern-looking bedding varieties, you could spoil the illusion of age. Look out for soft, subtle flowers.

WHAT YOU WILL NEED

• A ready painted terracotta trough
• Selection of plants chosen to colour-scheme with the container
• Crocks and gravel to cover drainage holes
• Trowel
• Potting mixture

1 Cover each drainage hole in the windowbox with a clay crock to prevent soil from being washed out during watering.

2 A layer of gravel for drainage is important if a terracotta container has been lined with plastic. Use a peat-based potting mix for summer bedding; a soil-based for permanent displays.

3 Pick a shade of *Impatiens* that tones with or complements the container. Here, a blush-pink busy Lizzie with a dark eye is teamed up with a deeper pink one. Interplant the front row with ivy.

Osteospermum 'African Summer'

Thymus × citriodorus 'Aureus'

Salvia officinalis 'Icterina'

Brachyscome multifida

left: *Variations on the theme: this pastel display is set off perfectly by the yellow paintwork of the terracotta trough. It demonstrates how simple it is to make a perfect match between container and plants.*

PAINTING A TERRACOTTA WINDOW BOX

Terracotta can look raw and orange when new. You can 'age' the surface quickly using a dilute colour wash of artist's acrylic. As the water is absorbed into the terracotta, an uneven and natural-looking covering of white pigment remains. This is how the pink finish was applied. Using diluted white artist's acrylic paint, roughly apply a wash to the surface of the dry terracotta container. The uneven coverage or drips are all part of the distressed look. Blot off the excess paint. Mix your colours together, here crimson and ultramarine, with some more white paint. Apply the paint in downward strokes.

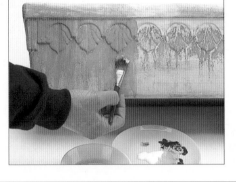

above: *Weathered terracotta works well with orange and green – here New Guinea hybrid impatiens, hart's tongue fern and variegated ground ivy combine.*

Impatiens F1 hybrid

4 This deep pink busy Lizzie picks up on the dark eye of the paler flower. Use it to fill in the gaps at the back, then work in more mix around each of the plants to cover the rootballs.

Hedera helix cultivar

5 This pastel display is perfect for shady walls. Other shade lovers include tuberous and fibrous-rooted begonias, bedding fuchsias, violas and *Lamium maculatum* 'White Nancy'.

Making a window box

WHAT YOU WILL NEED

- Tongued-and-grooved cladding, wood for a batten and a piece of roofing lathe
- Combination square, pencil, wood saw, tenon saw
- Drill and screwdriver (optional)
- Woodworking adhesive and panel pins, screws (optional)
- Hammer
- Stain, paint or preservative
- Plastic trough to act as a liner

Wooden planters and windowboxes are versatile and easy to build yourself in virtually any shape or size. The aim of this project is to make a wooden surround that will enclose a standard-sized plastic trough; these are widely available in a range of colours and sizes. Tongued-and-grooved cladding is an ideal material to make the sides of the windowbox; simply use as many planks as necessary to give the height of container you want. You can choose from several cladding profiles, but be sure to use the heavier weight 'structural' cladding rather than the thinner type supplied for facing surfaces. The one used here has a more detailed profile that gives the finished box more 'style'. There

Hybrid primroses

Narcissus 'Tête-à-Tête'

are two good reasons for using a plastic trough inside a wooden window-box. One is that the interior of the box is not in direct contact with the planting mixture and is therefore less liable to rot. The other is that it is easy to change the display by replacing the trough with another one planted up in a different way.

above: *A mixture of hybrid primroses and the early flowering dwarf daffodil, 'Tête-à-Tête' are combined here in a simple display. The impact is particularly strong because the yellow primrose centres and colour of the daffodils ties in so well with the window box.*

 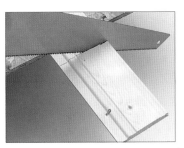  

1 Measure and mark the pieces of cladding that will form the end panels of the box. For a snug fit, make these 17cm(6.75in) wide.

2 Saw the end panels to length and sand the cut edges for a smooth finish. Each end panel will consist of two pieces of cladding.

3 Using a tenon saw, cut off the thinnest part of the tongue on the piece of cladding chosen to form the top of each end panel.

4 Squeeze some woodworking adhesive in the groove of the top piece of cladding and carefully push the two pieces together.

  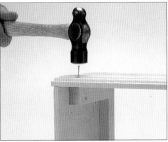 

5 Using panel pins, attach the bottom edge of the end panel to a batten cut to the same width. Use adhesive to create a firmer bond.

6 Cut long pieces of cladding and assemble them in pairs to make up the side panels. These should measure 63.5cm(25in).

7 Add adhesive and attach the side panels to the end panels with nails, creating a bottomless box that will fit around the trough.

8 Cut two pieces of roofing lathe to fit inside the box, sawing notches at each end so that they rest on the battens.

9 Push the support rails down onto the end battens. Screw them in place or leave them loose for removal when cleaning the box.

right: Plastic plant troughs can be very cheap to buy and make excellent waterproofing liners for wooden boxes.

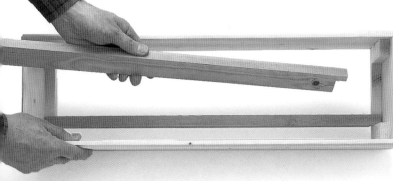 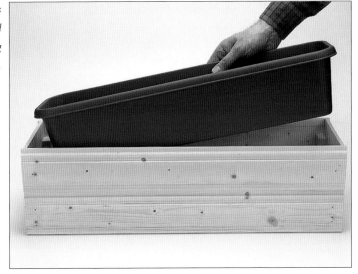

Decorating wooden troughs and window boxes

WHAT YOU WILL NEED

- A window box or planter made from wood or marine plywood
- Universal or wood primer and base coat to form the coloured backdrop for the stencilling, e.g. matt emulsion or artist's acrylic
- Paint brushes
- Stencil, stencil paint and stencil brush
- Masking tape
- Clear matt exterior varnish to seal the box

Nowadays you can create all kinds of different paint effects and there is no reason why you cannot apply interior design ideas to exterior items such as window boxes or wooden troughs. A plain painted or stained box allows greater flexibility when it comes to planting, but stencilled and free-hand painted designs add a touch of style. Create a more rustic finish to your window box by roughly applying paint so that you can see the brush marks clearly.

these pictures: *Attach the stencil with small pieces of masking tape. Use a stencil brush to pick up the paint (for this gothic design we have used gold), and then remove excess paint on paper. Apply in light circular movements, running over the edges of the stencil.*

VARIATION: STENCILLING

The good thing about stencilling is that it already has a somewhat weathered look and this suits items for the outdoor world. Choose a simple design and a single colour that will not compete with the plants. Then, either apply it all over the box in a random pattern or adopt a more formal approach – for example, by running a border across the middle of the box.

Impatiens F1 hybrid
(busy Lizzie)

Heuchera pulchella
'Rachel' (alum root)

Ajuga reptans
'Atropurpurea'

PRESERVING WOOD

Wooden boxes last longer if you use a plastic liner and treat the insides and underneath of the box itself with a penetrating wood preservative. Always check first that the preservative is safe for plants once it has dried. Alternatively, use a water-proof sealant. Before applying a topcoat of paint, seal with an aluminium primer.

above: *Cherry-red gloss paint applied in two coats over universal primer makes a very smart finish suitable for a town house. The planting has been chosen to enhance the red colouring with deep purple-black foliage.*

right: *A seaside feel has been achieved with a shell motif, silver and grey-leaved plants and a pebble mulch. Seal stencilling using a clear matt, exterior varnish. The plywood box below was roughly brushed over with a mix of acrylic paints to give it a weathered look.*

Translucent, water-based wood stains such as these are available in a range of bright colours. They allow the grain of the wood to show through.

STAINING A WOODEN WINDOW BOX

Some years ago, the only options for staining wood were varying shades of brown. Today, the range of stains and preservative paints is quite staggering. And what is more important, many are water-based, making them more pleasant to apply and safer to use with plants. Coordinate your plant displays with the colour of the container.

Verbena
'Blue Cascade'

Osteospermum
'Sunny Girl'

Senecio cineraria
'Silver Dust'

Helichrysum petiolare
'Variegatum'

Water Projects

A water feature in the garden is an instant focal point; the gleam of a pool, the sparkle of a fountain and the shapes and colours of lush water plants are irresistible. Once correctly installed, a water feature is easy to maintain, attracts a range of wildlife to the garden and is a constant source of interest and pleasure for you. It can transform your garden overnight, creating a relaxing retreat which also benefits nature.

In a small plot, 'conventional' ponds and water gardens are rarely practical. A pond needs to be a reasonable size for the water temperature to remain stable and the biological balance to 'work', keeping the water clean and fresh. There are, however, a number of different ways in which you can use water successfully in a limited space, without going to the trouble and expense of constructing a full-scale water garden.

Self-contained and child-safe features

below: A feature such as this millstone and cobble arrangement is perfectly safe for children because the reservoir containing the small submersible pump is concealed underground. All that's needed to complete the illusion is for the electric cable to be fed through armoured ducting and either buried or camouflaged with plants.

There are several situations where a conventional pool or pond may not be appropriate. Firstly, you may simply not have room to install one or it may be impossible to excavate the hole. Ponds may need more maintenance time than you are willing or able to spare. Another important consideration is that any depth of open water can be dangerous for small children.

A normal pond on a tiny scale needs a lot of maintenance to keep the water from turning green and to prevent pond and waterside plants clogging it. Otherwise it soon disappears from view or just looks a mess. But there are many ways to introduce water into a garden, apart from building a pond or an open-surfaced pool. Pebble pools, fountain and wall mask features that avoid any standing water are

below: Here an elegant vase spills over with water, the flow directed via four spouts into the shallow basin below. This is a good compromise when you do not have room for a pond but want to encourage birds to drink and bathe in your garden. When setting up this kind of feature, use a spirit level to ensure that the vessel is perfectly level so that the water falls evenly from each side.

Do:

• Introduce the sights and sounds of running water close to the house and around sitting areas
• Keep maintenance to a minimum by using self-contained water features
• Make cobble springs and other features where the reservoir is hidden away so that children can enjoy water in safety

Don't:

• Forget to use armoured cable for electrical connections to water features plus waterproof connectors. Always fit an RCD or circuit breaker
• Allow any depth of water where young children have access
• Site moving water features with a fountain in a windy spot. The pump may be damaged if it dries out

left: *You can use a millstone as a feature in its own right or to augment a larger pool or stream. When set in a bed of cobbles, make sure that the water flows back into the underground reservoir by lining the cobble area and reservoir with a complete sheet of butyl rubber. Use plastic tubing to connect the pump to the millstone.*

inherently low-maintenance and are perfectly safe for small children. Self-contained 'units' can be so compact and versatile they can be incorporated into even tiny or highly 'designed' gardens. Simply choose a style that goes with the rest of the garden. You can buy ready-to-install features that include a decorative architectural feature, such as a statue or urn complete with pump, reservoir and plumbing, or you can create your own design from the basic components. Another option is to make a small pool in a container. This can either be moved under cover in winter, or dismantled so that plants plus any fish can be kept indoors or in a heated greenhouse in winter to protect them from freezing.

Small formal pools

left: *Water lilies have fabulous flowers, which in the hardy varieties range in colour from white through pink to deep crimson red. They come in different size categories, so tell your supplier the depth of your pool and its approximate area and they will help you make an appropriate selection.*

Do:

• Use geometric shapes including circles for pools in formal or traditional gardens as well as modern urban sites
• Add a fountain or simple jet to create sound and movement and to help keep small pools in good health
• Use formal pools for ornamental fish or to grow plants like water lilies
• Camouflage the pool liner by creating a formal edging of paving

Don't:

• Allow water lilies and floating aquatic plants to cover more than a third of the water surface
• Use coloured liners; black pre-formed or butyl rubber liners give the best reflective quality for a pool.
• 'Clutter' a formal pool unnecessarily – keep surroundings simple
• Expect a formal pool to be a successful wildlife habitat

Pools with a regular geometric outline suit more formal gardens as well as those of an ultra-modern or minimalist design. Consider setting a small formal pool within a sunny paved terrace adjacent to the house or in a formal lawn or gravel area. The simplicity of a flat sheet of water works well in relatively spacious surroundings, but you can also mirror the shape of the pool with appropriately shaped flower borders or formal clipped hedging. Finish off with a dainty fountain spray or gushing spring feature that not only looks and sounds good but also helps to keep the water oxygenated and healthy.

You can often buy rigid pre-formed liners for this kind of pool. Simply excavate out the hole, bed the liner in position and camouflage the edge with paving stones or tiles. You can also use butyl rubber liner, but for a square or rectangular pool, the corners require careful folding to take up the excess. A pool with vertical sides and no shelving is unsuitable for wildlife, but ornamental fish and water lilies will be perfectly happy given sufficient depth.

A circular pool is not so severely formal as the straight-sided pool and a good compromise in a more relaxed setting. It is easy to mark out using a stake with a string attached that measures the same as the radius of the pool. Just push in markers at intervals as you walk around the stake keeping the string taut.

Encouraging wildlife with water

above: *Hostas and other moisture-loving perennials provide shelter for young frogs as they emerge from the pond.*

Water is like a magnet for wildlife. It attracts all manner of insects, amphibians, birds and small mammals and in so doing brings the garden to life. But to really be of value to wildlife, there are certain features that should be present in your pond, pool or stream.

In order for birds to drink and bathe safely there must be shallow water or a partially submerged perch for them to alight on, and the area must be fairly open so that they can keep an eye out for predators. Amphibians like frogs and toads also prefer a gently shelving access so that they can get in and out of the pool easily. This is particularly important when the tadpoles turn into adults and need to leave the water. At this point they are particularly vulnerable and their access should lead into an area of long grass or a bog garden with lush herbaceous planting for camouflage. Mammals like hedgehogs sometimes fall into ponds and can drown if there is no gently shelving access. Consider making a simple wooden ramp covered with galvanized wire mesh.

The health of the water is paramount, and it is important to site a wildlife pool in a relatively sunny spot away from deciduous trees. If fallen leaves are not removed, they can accumulate and rot, producing toxins. Establish oxygenators as soon as possible and build up marginal plantings to provide cover for aquatic animals and egg laying sites for dragonflies and damselflies. Water lily pads will help to shade the water, helping to minimise algal blooms.

above: *Making a home for frogs and toads is a good move if you want to control insects and slugs in your garden the natural way.*

FURTHER STEPS Although it will make the water pretty murky at first, it is a good idea to fill the base of the wildlife pond with garden soil before filling it with the hose. This will provide the plants and animals with essential nutrients. Animals will soon start to visit your pool, but you can get a good head start by 'seeding' the water from an established pond that already has a thriving aquatic community. Several weeks after the pond has been set up, add a couple of buckets of water and some sediment from the other pond. Avoid adding tap water to top up your pond, since the chemicals might upset the pond water chemistry and dissolved nitrates can cause algal blooms to occur.

Do:

• Provide safe, gently shelving access for birds, amphibians and other animals

• Ensure that the pool is well planted with lush vegetation to provide cover for animals and to attract insects to the area. The latter is particularly important if you want to lure dragonflies – they hunt other insects on the wing

• Allow the water to release dissolved chemicals like chlorine, before introducing plant life

Don't:

• Introduce ornamental fish to a wildlife pond. They have voracious appetites!

• Keep topping the pond up with tap water. It can upset the delicate balance

• Allow submerged or floating aquatics to choke the pond. Clear out excess once or twice a year avoiding frog spawning time

right: *This established pool is a mini wildlife sanctuary and contains all the elements required by the animals that visit it. It is also an attractive feature in its own right, due in part to the space that it has been allocated. There is enough room for marginal plantings and water lilies as well as open water.*

Raised pools and wall fountains

above: *This traditional terracotta wall mask would suit a formal garden with classical styling. The feature is completely self-contained with its own mini reservoir.*

A lovely way to create a tranquil corner is to build a raised pool that incorporates a bench seat. This brings the water and its plants and wildlife up to a height where they can easily be appreciated and allows you to sit on the edge and dangle your fingers in the water. Raised pools can be made using railway sleepers or other heavy pieces of sawn timber that simply stack on top of one another and are bolted together. Use a butyl liner and tuck the edges in underneath the top layer, using an industrial staple gun to hold it in place. A relatively inexpensive alternative is to use breeze blocks rendered with cement and painted with masonry paint to match other elements in the garden. Camouflage the top with timber seating, paving slabs or heavy terracotta tiles. Textured building blocks are more expensive and you can of course build raised pools from brick, but this really is a job for a professional. The advantage is that the pool could be made to fit in with other features in the garden and you could even create a pool on two levels using interlocking rectangles.

The wall mask or waterspout creates the illusion of a natural spring, where water flows constantly into a small pool below. Some self-contained units simply hang on the wall and there is

Do:

• Build seating into a raised pool and if possible combine it with existing garden features, e.g. a raised bed or retaining wall with steps
• Adjust the water flow coming out of a wall spout or mask so that it creates the right sound as it hits the reservoir below. Perhaps use a large cobble to break the fall before it hits the water surface
• Choose a wall mask design that's appropriate to the style of garden

Don't:

• Forget to disguise the water pipe that feeds the wall mask or to cover up the electric cable. The illusion is everything!
• Leave a small self-contained water fountain switched on when you are not around. The reservoir may run dry and cause the pump to burn out

above: *A modern rectangular raised pool creates a wonderful sitting area surrounded by flowers and foliage. The atmosphere is enhanced by the sight and sound of moving water in the shape of a ceramic cascade.*

left: *A contemporary water feature such as this would look well built into the terrace of a small city garden. Use a water-proofing bituminastic sealant on brickwork.*

no plumbing or pipe work to worry about. The disadvantage with this solution is that the reservoir is often very small and could dry out. This in turn could damage the tiny submersible pump if you are not careful and do not keep a close eye on the situation. You can create your own water reservoir that is completely child safe, using an underground tank covered with wire mesh and camouflaged with pebbles. However, if you do not want to dig a hole, use a wooden barrel to act as a pool instead. With the submersible pump in the reservoir, the plastic tubing that feeds the mask or spout needs to be camouflaged. Either chip a channel for it on the surface of the wall, afterwards covering it with mortar and then camouflaging it with plants such as ivy, or alternatively drill through the wall at the base and pass the tube through and up the other side.

A child-safe barrel pool

WHAT YOU WILL NEED

- Wooden half barrel (at least 60cm (24in) in diameter
- Pond liner
- Bricks and decorative pebbles, cobbles and boulders
- Small mains-powered submersible pump with bell fountain adaptor
- RCD or circuit breaker
- Marginal pond plants potted into pond planting baskets lined with plastic mesh or hessian

A bell fountain will fascinate children and adults alike and is easy to set up in a wooden half barrel. Using cobbles and pebbles you can hide the submersible pump and at the same time create a feature that is totally safe for young children because there is no depth of water. The feature shown here is just like a miniature pond complete with a variety of marginal plants. Most plants don't like to have their foliage constantly splashed by water, but here the water is contained within the shape of the bell fountain. Barrels have quite a rustic feel and work well in country and cottage-style gardens, but you could also use a glazed ceramic jar with the drainage hole blocked for a more modern or oriental feel.

1 Since the wooden barrel is not waterproof, line it with a large piece of pond liner. Push the liner firmly down inside. Trim off some of the excess but leave plenty around the edge.

2 Stand the pump on a hard brick for stability and to raise it up to the right level. This small mains-powered model is ideally suited to such a feature.

5 Add water until it reaches the base of the boulders. This will leave enough expansion room to add the plants and final stones. Do not dislodge the pump.

3 Add some cobbles to fill in the spaces between the bricks. These will help to stabilise the piles of bricks and will also stop the pump moving around once the feature is operating.

4 Now add the large stones that will form the visible part of the feature. Rounded boulders make an attractive contrast with the small pebbles.

Lysimachia thyrsiflora

Ranunculus flammula

Iris versicolor 'Blue Light'

Myosotis palustris

6 Add the plants, potted into plastic mesh pond baskets. Plan the planting in advance. A low-growing water forget-me-not towards the front will work well.

7 Add cobbles and pebbles to match the colour range and shape of the boulders. This helps the feature to look more like the bank of a natural stream. By now the barrel is very heavy and should be in its final location. Neaten the edge of the liner. Fit a bell fountain head to the pump outlet and switch on.

Epimedium × youngianum 'Roseum' *(Not a marginal but would look attractive close to the barrel.)*

Primula veris (Not suitable for inside the barrel.)

A miniature water lily pond

WHAT YOU WILL NEED

• A wooden barrel preferably
around 60cm (24in) in diameter.
Line with butyl rubber or heavy
duty polythene if not watertight
• A miniature water lily and two
other plants
• A sprig of Canadian pondweed
• Gravel and pebbles for the base
and to cover the soil in the
planting baskets
• Aquatic compost
• Four small goldfish

If you do not have room for a conventional pond, then a potted pond could be just the answer.
Put the container in position first, as it will be difficult to move once filled. You can use normal
tap water, but if possible fill the tub and allow it to stand for 48 hours before introducing plants.
This allows much of the chlorine to disperse. When choosing plants, opt for those with a long
season of interest. A single miniature water lily could be used alone; it will quickly fill a
45cm(18in)-diameter barrel with foliage, and flowers all summer. Or add up to two other plants.

**WATER LILIES FOR
A SMALL POOL**

You should use only the smallest
miniature water lilies for a barrel
pool, otherwise the planting will
be completely out of scale and
the water lily will spill out over
the edges. Site the pool in full
sun, otherwise the plants will
not thrive and the flowers will
not open up. Visit a good water
gardening specialist for the best
range of plants. Two excellent
varieties are *Nymphaea
pygmaea* 'Helvola', a very free-
flowering miniature with tiny
star-shaped pale yellow flowers
and red-marbled olive-green
leaves and *N.* 'Laydekeri
Purpurata', with small marbled
leaves that set off deep pink
flowers produced all summer.

VARIATIONS ON THE THEME

Why not make a group of potted ponds? Use matching containers in various sizes, each with a
different planting theme. You might have a water lily pond; a marginal plant pond; a bog garden; a
fountain-and-pebble pond or a floating garden with water hyacinth.

1 Use a waterproof wooden barrel, or line it first with thick black plastic or butyl rubber pond liner. Half-fill it with water and add a tall, strikingly shaped, leafy plant, such as this miniature umbrella plant.

2 Choose a second plant that complements the first; foliage types look good all season. Slowly submerge the planting baskets. Covering the aquatic compost with gravel helps keep the water clear.

3 To oxygenate the water for the fish, add a sprig of Canadian pondweed (*Elodea canadensis*), securing it on the bottom with a cobble. It is evergreen so keeps working in winter.

4 Lower the water lily slowly, protecting the leaves and flowers, which become weak and floppy out of water. They easily tear if snagged on the edge of the barrel. Stand the pot on the bottom.

5 Four small fish are plenty for a barrel this size. Float their bag on the surface for 30 minutes so that their water reaches the same temperature as that in the tub. Open the neck of the bag under water, allowing the fish to swim out.

Schoenoplectus 'Zebrinus' (zebra rush)

Cyperus involucratus (umbrella plant)

6 After a few hours, the lily leaves shrug off water and emerge floating on the pond surface. Water lily flowers only open fully in direct sun, so make sure the pond is correctly sited from the very start.

Choose a miniature water lily that will thrive in shallow water.

Setting up a water pump

Skill level:

DIY electrical wiring

experience useful

Best time to do:

Mid- to late spring,

ready for the season

ahead

Special tools required:

Hammer action drill

Time required:

Allow half a day

WHAT YOU WILL NEED

• Submersible pump with filter
attachment and waterfall/
fountain t-piece adaptor
• RCD or circuit breaker to cut
power instantly if a fault is
detected
• Fountain head fixture
• Waterproof on/off switch
• Tools, including hammer action
drill to allow wiring through the
wall of the garage or house

A submersible pump is quite powerful enough for most small water features. The smallest models are little bigger than a fist and as long as they can be covered by water, can run in as little as half a gallon. You will need a larger, more powerful pump if the water has to be raised any height to run a waterfall or a fountain raised up on top of a statue. Some types of fountain jet (such as the popular bell jet) need more power to provide sufficient through-flow of water to run them. Check before buying a pump that it is capable of powering the sort of feature you have in mind. If you want a fountain you will need to attach a special fitment to the outlet pipe from the pump.

1 If you want to use the built-in filter, simply push it over the inlet pipe of the pump until it clicks into place. It is easy to remove for cleaning. The built-in filter houses a block of plastic filter foam.

Adjusting screw regulates the upward flow.

The water will flow up this pipe.

This outlet is blanked off, so the water will flow upwards.

2 If you plan to run a fountain and perhaps a waterfall as well, push the T-piece adapter onto the outlet pipe of the pump. Screw on a blanking cap if you decide not to run a waterfall from the adaptor. Fit a tube if you change your mind.

3 The pump is ready to have a fountain head fitted on top of the outlet pipe. The built-in foam pad will filter the water as it is sucked through the vents in the casing.

4 Fit the T-piece into the top outlet and select a fountain head. The one with three circles of holes produces a three-tier pattern with a wide spread of water.

above: *In this romantic scene, water spills from an overturned jar into the pond thanks to a hidden submersible pump.*

VARIATIONS: BUBBLE OR GEYSER

The geyser head produces a strong jet of aerated water. To get the best effect, operate the pump at its most powerful setting. Correctly adjusted, a bell fountainhead produces a smooth, symmetrical dome of water. To change the shape, push in the cone at the top of the head and starting low, gradually increase the water flow.

Water features using hidden reservoirs

Skill level:

Beginner gardener

Best time to do:

Anytime

Special tools required:

An electric drill

Time required:

Allow a couple of hours

once materials have

been assembled

Water bubbling up out of the ground like a spring can be an intriguing effect. To make a feature like this, first excavate a hole big enough to take an underground reservoir. A plastic cold-water tank from a plumber's merchants is ideal but you can also use a large sheet of butyl liner over a base of soft sand. Place the submersible pump in the reservoir; connect plastic tubing to the outlet so that it passes through the hole in your drilled pebble or millstone. Alternatively fit a geyser attachment to give the effect of a bubbling spring emerging from a bed of pebbles. To support this kind of surface camouflage, use a sheet of rigid wire mesh that overlaps the edge of the reservoir.

A POTTED FOUNTAIN Set up a potted fountain with care. Make sure that the pot, stones, etc., are all perfectly clean, as any dirt and grit will soon clog the pump. The submersible pump must be covered by water at all times. Adjust the jet so that the water trickles back into the pot and is continuously recycled – if too high, much of the water will go over the sides of the container. If the container empties, the pump runs dry and will be damaged. Top up the water level at least once a week, since evaporation will gradually lower the water level. A small bubble fountain like this only needs the smallest type of submersible pump; choose a low voltage one, and plug it into an RCD.

WHAT YOU WILL NEED

• Plastic terracotta or stone-effect patio planter
• Electric drill
• Small submersible pump
• Wire hanging basket minus chains
• Piece of wire to secure outlet tube
• Length of plastic tubing that fits snugly over pump outlet
• Pebbles or cobbles depending on size of feature

1 Use a tiny pump that will work in a small quantity of water. Attach clear plastic tubing to the nozzle and sit the pump in the pot. Drill a hole under the pot rim and thread the wire through.

2 Find a hanging basket frame the right size to sit inside the pot, covering the pump. Remove the chains and fit it firmly in place so it will not slip when weighted down with pebbles.

3 Wire the tip of the nozzle to the framework of the basket to hold it securely. There is no need to fit a spray head, as the nozzle alone will produce a clean natural-shaped jet of water.

left: *A large boulder with a hole drilled through sits above a concealed water reservoir. This arrangement is ideal for an oriental or Zen garden.*

above: *You can add a special jet to the outlet at the top of the pump to produce a formal bell fountain.*

4 Part-fill the container with water, covering the pump completely, with 5cm(2in) to spare. This ensures that the pump will remain covered with water when the fountain is in operation. Hide the pump and the hanging basket pump cover completely under a layer of smooth clean pebbles; choose a size of pebble that is in proportion to the size of the container.

5 When the pump is switched on, a simple fountain effect trickles water over the pebbles. Adjust the pump valve to make the fountain jet a suitable height.

Installing a pond

Skill level:

This is not a difficult

task, but it is physically

demanding

Best time to do:

In warm weather. The

heat makes the liner

more flexible and

easier to fit

Special tools required:

None

Time required:

A whole weekend

An important element in the success of a pond is its liner. With rigid, pre-formed liners you are limited by the choice of shape, but with flexible liners, there are no such restrictions. Materials vary in price according to durability. If possible, avoid the coloured liners, particularly for naturalistic features and for pools where the reflective quality of the water is key. The best liner you can buy – and this is available in different grades – is butyl rubber. It is normally guaranteed for at least 10 years. It is thick and consequently heavy, so for a large pool you will need some assistance to put it in position.

Inexpensive polythene material in black, blue, brown and green.

PVC blend with a high plasticiser content to improve flexibility and durability. Also 0.5mm(0.02in) thick.

EPDM (ethylene propylene diene rubber membrane)1mm (0.04in) thick. Very durable.

PVC (polyvinyl chloride) liner 0.5mm(0.02in) thick for smaller pools only.

LDPE (low-density polyethylene) liner 0.02in(0.5mm) thick.

These are non-woven polyester underlays for cushioning the liner.

Butyl (isobutylene isoprene rubber) 0.75mm (0.03in) thick. Very strong and long lasting.

HOW MUCH LINER?

Pools vary in size; to calculate the amount of liner you will need, add twice the maximum depth of the pool to both the overall length and width. Thus, a 3x1.8x0.6m (10ftx 6ftx2ft) deep pool needs a liner 4.2x3m(14x10ft). Liner is flexible and stretches to fit with the weight of the water, so there is no need to allow for gentle contouring.

USING RIGID LINERS The easiest type of liners to buy are the preformed pools, available in a limited choice of sizes and in both formal and informal styles from any good garden centre. Most

of these moulded pools incorporate a marginal shelf for plants. Rigid pools are also available in much thicker plastic and even stronger, but more expensive, are the preformed GRP (glass reinforced plastic) shapes. You can make a formal raised pool quite easily using a rigid liner well supported with breezeblocks, the exposed sides camouflaged with paving slabs or similar.

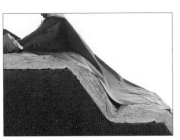

1 To protect the liner against damage from sharp stones etc., use soft pond underlay or a thick layer of soft sand.

2 Lay the pool liner over the excavated hole, taking care that there is an equal amount of excess around the outside.

3 Anchor the edges of the liner with smooth slabs, boulders or bricks. You can move these around as the pool fills with water.

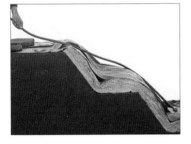

4 Now fill the pool slowly using a hosepipe to produce a steady trickle of water. The weight of the water will pull the liner into place.

5 When the pool has filled to its level, cut away any excess liner, leaving about 30cm(12in) to be anchored and hidden by your choice of edging.

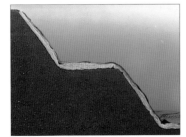

6 This profile represents a small liner pool filled for the first time. Leave the pond to settle for a day or two before completing the edging.

POOL EDGING IDEAS

There are several ways of edging a garden pool. The aim is to provide access to the water and to soften and disguise the junction of the pool liner and the surrounding garden. Here are a few options.

Turf edging produces a natural look and is easy to lay. The pool liner can be anchored beneath the soil and turves.

Grass, with stone slabs set on sand at intervals around the edge and slightly overlapping the water, hide and anchor the liner.

Brick edging that slightly overlaps the pool needs good foundations: a 15cm(6in) layer of hardcore, 2.5cm(1in) of sand and 2.5cm (1in) of cement.

Paving slabs have a larger surface area to spread the weight of people walking on them. Lay a 7.5cm(3in) layer of hardcore to give stability.

Unless you want to create a natural sloping beach running into the pool, contain an edging of pebbles with wooden battens to prevent erosion.

Oxygenating and floating plants

WHAT YOU WILL NEED

• Plastic perforated planting basket
• A bag of aquatic soil (this contains very little organic matter)
• Bunches of oxygenating plants to grow submerged
• Washed gravel or small pebbles
• Hessian or plastic mesh sheets – these may be needed to contain the soil if the slits in the basket sides are large

A selection of oxygenating plants is essential for the good health of your pool, especially if the pond is new. These are mostly submerged, or occasionally floating, species of water plants that use up waste nutrients in the water by means of their underwater foliage. This, and the fact that such plants grow prolifically, will quickly deprive bothersome algae of nutrients and minerals, and thus help to keep the water clean. They not only prevent green water and blanketweed, but also provide useful cover for pond insects and small fish. For the average pool, you will need about five oxygenating plants per square metre (one per two square feet) of surface area. Larger pools, over 14 square metres (150 square feet), can reduce that requirement to nearer three bunches per square metre (one per three square feet). Different species flourish at different times of year, so a selection of at least two or three species is the most successful way to beat murky water. Floating plants are unrooted and float on, or just below, the water surface. Most require a water depth of 30-90cm(12-36in) and are easy to install, simply by resting the plant gently on the surface.

PLANTING OXYGENATORS

1 Fill a perforated container with aquatic soil almost to the rim. Make a series of planting holes with your fingers or a dibber and position the plants evenly around the container.

2 When all the plants are firmed in, top up the container with a layer of washed gravel or small stones to anchor the potting mix and to prevent fish from rooting out the plants.

above: *the tiny, semi-evergreen leaves of* Lagarosiphon major *(also known as* Elodea crispa*) are clustered along each stem.*

above: Fontinalis antipyretica *thrives in sun or semi-shade and prefers running water, such as a stream.*

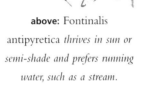

left: Hottonia palustris *makes a clump of feathery, light green leaves, with tall spikes of pale lilac or white flowers in summer.*

above: Ranunculus aquatilis *has bright green feathery foliage that can become invasive if not kept in check.*

above: Ceratophyllum demersum *grows best in cool water; it spreads to make a submerged mat of tiny dark green leaves.*

left: *Annual* Trapa natans *is grown for its attractive leaves, white summer flowers and edible nuts.*

below: Pistia stratiotes, *a tender perennial, needs tropical or subtropical conditions.*

FLOATING PLANTS

It is not generally recommended that you put prolific floating plants into very large ponds unless you can devise some means of removing them, as they could soon dominate the feature.

below: *In sunny, lime-rich waters the water soldier (Stratiotes aloides) flourishes. It produces tiny white flowers all summer amongst floating rosettes of narrow pointed leaves.*

above: Eichhornia crassipes, *the water hyacinth, is a tender glossy evergreen with large violet-blue flowers.*

above: *To plant a water soldier (Stratiotes aloides), simply place it in the water. It is remains submerged at first then rises to the surface.*

Choosing marginal plants

WHAT YOU WILL NEED

• Plastic perforated planting basket
• A bag of aquatic soil
• Marginal plants – one large/vigorous or two or three smaller plants per basket. Don't mix different types together.
• Washed gravel or small pebbles
• Hessian or plastic mesh sheets – these may be needed to contain the soil if the slits in the basket sides are large

The plants that grow along the banks and shallows of ponds and streams are among the most dramatic and beautiful species you could wish to feature in your garden. As a group, they include a wonderful variety of size, shape and colour within the range of their foliage alone, while some have spectacular flowers, too, at certain times of the year. These plants are usually positioned on the marginal shelf, specially built just below the surface of the water, so that these mud-loving plants can keep their roots waterlogged. You can plant them directly onto the shelf in soil enriched with humus or pot them up into specially perforated plastic baskets for easy maintenance. It is not a good idea to plant marginals all the way around the pool, as this would totally obscure the pool itself and deny you access to the water's edge. It is more usual to plant up about one-third of the circumference.

above: *Buy small pots of marginal plants from a good water garden supplier and pot up into larger perforated baskets to develop.*

1 Fill the basket with moist aquatic potting mixture and plant two or three plants of the same type in it. Backfill and firm in. Add a layer of gravel.

2 Holding the container firmly by the handles on both sides, lower it gently onto the marginal shelf without disturbing the water too much.

CHOOSING PLANTS

Ponds and water gardens offer a unique opportunity to grow plants that need to be grown in, on or by water. Make the most of their fascinating personalities and enjoy the new range of wildlife they attract to the garden.

MOISTURE-LOVING PLANTS

Anemone rivularis
Aruncus dioicus
'Glasnevin'
Arundo donax
'Versicolor'
Astilbe
Cardamine pratensis
Cornus alba 'Sibirica'
Filipendula ulmaria
Geum rivale
Gunnera manicata
Hosta
Iris ensata (I. kaempferi)
'Alba'
 'Variegata'
 I. hoogiana 'Hula Doll'
 I. innominata 'Irish Doll'
  'Jack o' Hearts'
 I. sibirica 'Sparkling Rose'
 Ligularia dentata 'Desdemona'
 L. przewalskii 'The Rocket'
Lobelia cardinalis 'Queen Victoria'
 Lythrum salicaria
 Osmunda regalis
 Parnassia palustris
Peltiphyllum peltatum
Petasites japonicus
Phalaris arundinacea 'Picta'
Primula denticulata, P. japonica,
 P. pulverulenta, P. veris, P. vulgaris
Rheum alexandrae, R. palmatum
Rodgersia pinnata 'Superba'
Scrophularia auriculata 'Variegata'
Trollius x cultorum 'Canary Bird'
 T. chinensis 'Golden Queen'

MARGINAL PLANTS

Acorus calamus 'Variegatus'
Calla palustris
Caltha palustris 'Flore Pleno'
Carex elata 'Aurea', *C. pendula*
Cyperus longus
Eupatorium cannabinum, E. purpureum
Glyceria maxima 'Variegata'
 G. spectabilis 'Variegata'
Houttuynia cordata 'Chameleon'
 'Flore Pleno'
Iris ensata (I. kaempferi)
 I. laevigata
 I. pseudacorus 'Variegata'
 I. versicolor 'Blue Light'
Juncus effusus
 J.e. spiralis
Lysichiton americanus
Lysimachia nummularia 'Aurea'
Mentha aquatica
Mimulus guttatus
 M. luteus 'Nana'
Myosotis scorpioides, M. palustris
Myriophyllum verticillatum
Orontium aquaticum
Pontederia cordata
Sagittaria sagittifolia 'Flore Pleno'
Scirpus albescens, S. zebrinus
Typha latifolia 'Variegata'
 T. minima
Zantedeschia aethiopica

FLOATING PLANTS

Azolla filiculoides
Eichhornia crassipes
Hydrocharis morsus-ranae
Lemna triscula
Pistia stratiotes
Utricularia vulgaris

OXYGENATING PLANTS

Callitriche hermaphroditica (C. autumnalis)
 C. palustris (C. verna)
Ceratophyllum demersum
Eleocharis acicularis, E. palustris
Elodea canadensis
Lagarosiphon major (Elodea crispa)
Potamogeton crispus
Ranunculus aquatilis
Stratiotes aloides

DEEP WATER PLANTS

Aponogeton distachyos
Nymphaea (Water lilies)

Planting water lilies

For many pond owners, the large lily pad leaves and beautiful lotus-like blooms of the water lily are the epitome of a water garden. There is such a wonderful variety of types, offering different colours, forms and even scent. However, it is important to choose varieties with care, as the large, vigorous types are totally unsuitable for smaller pools. It is easy to be tempted to grow lots of different types, but lilies don't like to be crowded and can easily swamp the water surface. The plants will look much better given space to appreciate the leaf shape.

PLANTING A WATER LILY Water lilies are greedy feeders, especially the more vigorous types, so provide the largest container possible and a soil depth of at least 15cm(6in). Containers include perforated baskets and wide, solid-sided bowls. Transplant lilies in spring so that they can establish themselves before the dormant season.

WHAT YOU WILL NEED

• Plastic perforated planting basket
• A bag of aquatic soil
• Water lily plants – one per basket
• Washed gravel or small pebbles
• Hessian or plastic mesh sheets – these may be needed to contain the soil if the slits in the basket sides are large
• Bricks to raise the basket up to the correct level

1 Lay the lily onto the potting mixture and top up the basket with more mixture, firming in the plant as you proceed.

2 Cover the surface with gravel or small stones to keep the soil in place once the basket is lowered into the water.

3 Place bricks in the pool to bring the basket to the right level below the water surface. See label for planting depth.

WATER LILY SIZES It is vital to choose a water lily that suits the size of your pond. This table is a guide to the eventual spread of different sizes of water lilies and the recommended planting depths.		Spread	Planting depth
	Miniature	0.09m² (1ft²)	10-23cm (4-9in)
	Small	0.3m² (3ft²)	15-38cm (6-15in)
	Moderate	0.6-1.1m² (6-12ft²)	15-45cm (6-18in)
	Medium	1.1-1.3m² (12-14ft²)	15-60cm (6-24in)
	Large	1.3-2.3m² (14-26ft²)	23-120cm (9-48in)

4 Lower the container into the water so that it rests on the bricks. Do not drop it in; you may damage the plant and pond liner.

5 If it has been correctly planted, the lily leaves will eventually float up to rest on the water surface. Place young plants in shallow water at first.

right: *Tropical water lilies with their clear violet or blue flowers are magical, but they will have to be brought in under cover at the end of the season. A conservatory pool is ideal.*

Installing fountains and waterfalls

Skill level:

Keen gardener or DIY

enthusiast with

experience of garden

constructions and

electrics

Best time to do:

Any mild spell

Special tools required:

None

Time required:

May take a couple of

weekends

The splash and glitter of a fountain adds excitement and allure to even the smallest pool. Once you have put in the pump, all you need is a fountain nozzle or jet, a length of plastic tubing and jubilee clips to connect them. Nozzles and jets range from tall plumes and multiple spray sequences to a simple bell or dome suitable for smaller pools. An ornamental device such as a spouting fish or abstract sculpture could be carefully positioned to hide the mechanism.

A waterfall or cascade can also be used to introduce the sight and sound of moving water. It need not be a large feature; indeed, too tall a waterfall would require a tremendous volume of water and a very powerful pump to keep it circulating. Even a trickle from one formal patio pool into another slightly below it, makes a delightful feature. A rocky waterfall cascading over boulders into an informal pond gives a naturalistic effect that needs careful placing to be convincing. Use the waste stone and soil from your pool excavations to achieve a slope on flat ground. Select a pump powerful enough to cope with the required

WHAT YOU WILL NEED

• Submersible pump
• Waterfall/fountain adaptor
• Detachable filter
• Butyl rubber liner
• Length of tubing to carry water to the top of the cascade
• Flat stone slabs to line the cascade and form 'steps'
• Plants, pebbles and stones for camouflage
• Bricks to raise pump up off base of pond

Position the spray fountainhead just above water level. A delicate fountain is a refreshing sight, but a simple jet works well in a contemporary setting.

Control the height of the fountain by adjusting the water flow regulator. Make sure that water does not fall outside the pool.

Raise the pump on bricks to bring the fountain head to the correct level. This also helps to prevent the pond sucking in debris from the bottom of the pool.

volume of water and the height of the falls; if you have already installed one of the larger types to run a fountain or other moving water feature, it may be possible to use the pump to run both features by adding a T-piece to the outlet pipe. Let your stockist advise you on the equipment you might need. If the waterfall is a big one, you may also need a header tank or pool to maintain a large enough water supply.

If you just want to run a waterfall, simply connect a suitable length of plastic tubing directly to the outlet of a submersible pump (as shown here) and direct the water flow as you wish. Remember to camouflage the cable and plastic tubing to maintain the illusion.

Here the tubing is left exposed, but in the garden camouflage it so that water appears to spring from the stones.

The maximum size of fountain depends on the height of the waterfall and the length of tubing involved. Ask your supplier to help you with the necessary calculations.

Block off the other unused outlets on your pump using a blanking cap. It will run more efficiently as a result.

In this set-up, a submersible pump supplies water to a spray fountain and a waterfall. Make sure that the pump you choose can power both outlets.

above: *An informal style cascade built up from slabs of stone needs a liner beneath it to prevent the water soaking into the surrounding soil and emptying the pond. Give a generous overlap between the liner used for the pool and that of the cascade, as water will always find a way of working up between gaps.*

Making a bog garden

Skill level:

Beginner gardener

Best time to do:

Mid-spring to early

summer when a good

selection of plants is

available

Special tools required:

None

Time required:

Allow at least one day

WHAT YOU WILL NEED

• Sheet of pond liner or heavy
duty polythene
• A garden fork
• Gravel
• Bricks or boulders to hold
liner in place temporarily
• Length of perforated hose
• Aquatic planting mix
• Selection of moisture-loving
plants
• Decorative boulders and
cobbles

The beauty of creating a bog or marsh area in the garden is that it offers you the chance to grow a wider range of exciting marginal plants. Or you may welcome the chance to establish a rewarding water feature without the need for expensive excavation work. Ideally, the site should be sheltered from prevailing winds with a little, but not too much, shade. The most natural position is adjoining the banks of an informal pond or pool, but if you are planning an individual bog garden, then any slight depression or poorly drained area will be ideal. It is important to keep the area poorly drained and to make allowances for fluctuations in the water level according to the differing levels of rainfall throughout the year. Avoid positioning the bog garden too near any tree.

left: *A bog garden creates a completely different growing environment in which to grow moisture-loving plants, even if you don't have a pool. The combination of lush foliage and cobbles creates the illusion of a stream side and you can strengthen that illusion by installing a bubbling spring feature.*

Mimulus

1 Excavate the area to a depth of about 35cm(14in), level the base and spread out a large sheet of pond lining material. Anchor it with a few large, smooth boulders. Puncture the bottom of the liner a couple of times with a garden fork, so that some water can escape later on. Add a layer of washed gravel.

2 Lay a section of pipe, perforated at 30cm(12in) intervals, on the gravel. Allow the end to extend beyond the bog garden area and conceal it in the undergrowth.

3 In dry spells, trickle water into the pipe as needed. Fill the area to the original ground level with rich, moisture-retaining, aquatic planting mixture.

4 Soak the ground thoroughly, so that a layer of water about 7.5cm(3in) deep remains standing on the top of the soil before you start putting in any plants. It all needs to be very wet.

5 Position the plants so that they are at the same depth as they were in their pots. Firm them in. Hostas such as this have great shape and colour possibilities. Arrange more delicate plants, such as primulas, in clumps. Aim for a variety of shape, size and colour for year-round plant interest.

Lysimachia thyrsiflora

Astilbe

Lobelia cardinalis

Primula veris

Hosta

Pipe left accessible for watering.

Making a wildlife water feature

Skill level:

Beginner gardener

Best time to do:

Anytime, but probably

best to avoid working

in wet weather

Special tools required:

None

Time required:

Most of a weekend,

depending on the size

of the feature

WHAT YOU WILL NEED

• Watertight barrel or butyl liner
for a larger feature
• Boulders, cobbles, pebbles –
different sizes of stones according
to the nature of the feature you
wish to create
• A varied selection of marginal
and moisture-loving plants
• Spade
• Garden fork
• Trowel

It takes surprisingly little water to attract wildlife into a garden. A sunken barrel pond measuring only 60cm(24in) across, containing oxygenating plants and two or three marginals will soon become a home for frogs, especially in the heat of summer. Put in a rounded boulder raised up on bricks so that birds have somewhere to perch and the mini pond will have even more visitors. An adjacent bog garden will extend the wildlife refuge, providing moist cover for animals such as young frogs and toads and if you are very fortunate, newts.

Increasing the volume of water will draw in far more insects, birds and animals. If possible, allocate quite a large area to relatively shallow water with a gently shelving 'beach'. A deeper area of water, to at least 1m (3ft), will ensure the survival of aquatic animals over winter. Although the area for bird drinking and bathing needs to be quite open, the rest of the pool margin should be densely planted and a large proportion of the aquatic plants, marginals and moisture-lovers should consist of native plants. Use black butyl rubber lining for a long-lasting pool with natural contouring.

left: *Amphibians like toads and frogs are sure to use the wildlife pond and its surroundings, but depending on the area in which you live, you may also have surprise residents or temporary visitors such as newts, grass snakes and slow worms. Piles of rocks adjacent to the pool will increase the habitat for these animals spending time out of water.*

right: *Life above and below the pool surface is fascinating. Pond skaters like the one illustrated glide over the water. Dragonflies and damselflies dart to and fro, attracted by the large numbers of insects that form their prey and, below the surface, diving beetles, dragonfly nymphs and a whole host of creatures go about their business. All maintain the delicate ecological balance of the pool.*

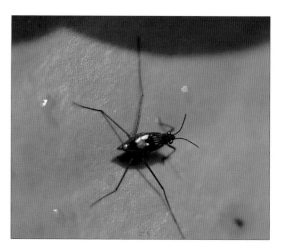

left: *A natural looking stream side effect has been created here, using cobbles that spread from the bank right down into the water. This is an ideal way to hide the liner and makes a useful habitat for small aquatic creatures. Notice how the iris clumps, reeds, rushes and ornamental grasses add to the waterside feel and make the pool area look as though it is part of a wild landscape.*

MAKING A COBBLE BEACH A cobble beach like the one illustrated is not hard to establish. Provided you use a proper heavy-duty liner such as butyl rubber, you can lay stones and cobbles on top of it quite safely. Avoid stones with sharp edges that could puncture the liner if walked on, and for very large stones, for example stepping-stones, place these on folded layers of pond liner and soft underlay to cushion the load. Use different grades of rounded boulders, cobbles and pebbles to create a more natural look, similar to that found on a streamside.

Finishing Touches

The garden can be a place for self-expression and for creating your very own works of art. You do not necessarily have to spend very much money on this as the pictures to the left demonstrate. Just have some fun and experiment with different ideas and materials. The finishing touches that make a garden special and which add a personal note might range from painting a garden seat, to weaving your own decorative plant supports or hanging wind chimes and candle lanterns from a pergola. If you decide to save up and buy a more expensive item such as a large ceramic jar or a piece of classical statuary, you will want to make the most of it. But that does not necessarily mean giving it pride of place; in a garden the subtle approach is often far more effective.

Creating garden focal points

below: Outdoor decorations can be great fun and can bring a lot of individual character to a garden. Whether these faces represent the garden owners is unknown, but the quirky design and plain backdrop certainly make them stand out. Larger garden centres also sell a wide range of wall plaques and masks.

Before you go out and spend a lot of money on an ornament, it is a good idea to experiment. It can be very difficult to judge the ideal size and shape needed to fit a particular space unless you do this. Use piled up cardboard boxes to estimate the size of a classical urn on a pedestal, or an ordinary plastic dustbin to stand in for a large Chinese jar. Ornamental constructions like archways can be tried out using long bamboo canes lashed together, and why not make cardboard cut-outs to represent a statue? This will not only help you to gauge the size needed, but will also make it easier to work out the exact placing. It is a lot easier to move a piece of cardboard around than it is a heavy stone ornament!

In very small gardens it is tempting to stick to small pots and ornaments that seem in proportion with the space, but the reverse strategy can often make the garden feel larger and more relaxed.

right: This classical urn is perfectly placed. The long straight path leads the eye straight to it and the trellis walkway creates tunnel vision. Notice too how the clipped hedge backdrop provides a simple contrasting foil for the paler urn. Imagine what this view would be like if there was nothing for the eye to focus on or if the urn was smaller.

Do:

• Experiment with substitute objects first before buying or placing a real garden ornament

• Create an appropriate backdrop for the object or focal point

• Use pathways, the curve of a lawn or border and arches to set up sightlines to your focal point

• Give smaller objects greater prominence by raising them up from ground level for example

Don't:

• Clutter the garden with too many features. There should be space to appreciate each one fully.

• Forget that one large pot can have far more impact in a small space than lots of little ones

• Mix too many different styles – pick a theme

left: *Here several elements are brought together to create a pleasing focus for the corner of a garden. The main focus and visual 'anchor' for the composition comes from the large jar with its simple outline. The elegant table and chair are relatively light visually and would not be such a draw to the eye without the ceramic jar. The plain brick wall and gravel surface provide a suitable backdrop.*

below left: *Garden sculptures can be made from all kinds of materials whether natural or man-made. They can be abstract – such as piles of weathered terracotta pots and this pebble sculpture or figurative like the faces opposite. Small pieces need very careful placing so that they are not lost in the general context of the garden.*

Instead of filling the garden with a clutter of small pots, consider one really big terracotta or glazed jar. It will have far more impact. The right backdrop is vital. The more delicate and finely wrought the object, the greater the need for a simple, contrasting background – a plain wall or the dark green foliage of a climber. In formal gardens, paths and walkways are used to set up the sightline so that the eye instantly focuses on the ornament or feature at the end. Pergolas and arches amplify that effect. In an informal garden, enhance existing focal points such as a pool and place solid objects like sculptures and pots in amongst the flowers.

Using colour effectively

The way you use colour in the garden can have a tremendous effect on the success of your design. We are happy to consider colour scheming indoors, but out in the garden we often jumble colours together and the effects can be far from relaxing. At the other end of the scale are virtual monochrome plantings, such as white gardens. These are much harder to create than you might imagine and there is always a danger that they will turn out rather dull and uninteresting.

The main element of any garden colour scheme is green. There are a myriad shades and some incredibly tranquil gardens such as certain Japanese styles employ this colour very successfully, using other colours only sparingly.

Colour affects our mood and can also give a certain look or feel to a garden. The use of lots of grey and silver foliage, white, blue and a few yellow flowers can create a seaside feel, especially when combined with gravel and pebbles. Terracotta coloured pots, tiles and rendering suggests a hot climate even before the plants have been added. Bright reds, oranges and dayglow colours like magenta and cerise stimulate, whilst soft mauves and purples create a quieter, more contemplative atmosphere.

You can change the feel of the garden and make the various parts more interesting by contrasting the colour schemes used in different parts. This is particularly effective in a segmented garden consisting of a series of outdoor rooms. To lift schemes that use closely related colours, drop in spots of contrasting or complementary colours, for example, in an all yellow and cream border, use lavender blue or purple highlights and in a pastel pink planting consider deep velvety crimson.

right: *You can get away with a broad mix of colours – here, pink, yellow, orange and red – provided you have a calming backdrop of blue and green foliage. The wide expanse of stone paving also acts as a neutral foil.*

Do:

• Use colour scheming to create different moods and effects in the garden remembering that greens are neutral, hot colours stimulate and cool colours relax

• Use contrasting colours to highlight certain features or objects, e.g. set a blue-painted chair against a backdrop of an all yellow planting

• Link colour schemes indoors and out to create the illusion of space

Don't:

• Use too many different colours together, especially in a small space, unless the backdrop is neutral, e.g. a white wall or a soft blue-grey painted fence

• Be too rigid with colour scheming – the effects can be rather flat

• Overdo colour contrasts. They work best as occasional highlights

• Use very bright, attention grabbing colours like white and orange at the end of a small garden. It will make the space feel even shorter. To lengthen the garden, use softer blues, purples and greys

Effects with glass beads and chippings

Skill level:

Some experience of

creating water features

useful

Best time to do:

Anytime

Special tools required:

None

Time required:

Allow the whole

weekend, to include

time for excavating

the depression

WHAT YOU WILL NEED

- Tools to dig the pool out with
- Pond liner, e.g. butyl rubber
- Soft sand and pond underlay to create a cushioned base for the liner
- Sacks of differently coloured glass chippings
- Evergreen ornamental grasses and sedges
- Sculpture or water spout connected to a small, hidden submersible pump

New materials continue to appear at the forefront of design and one such novel product that has now filtered through to the garden centres is the glass chip or bead. Chips are mainly used as an alternative surfacing material in place of gravel and pebbles. Glass chips come in subtle ice colours as well as deep blue or green and are a bi-product of glass recycling. All the sharp edges have been ground down so that they are quite safe to handle. In the garden they enhance ultra-modern, minimalist schemes, but because of their glittering transparency they can also be used to create magical, otherworldly effects. Glass chips work best in quite limited areas and are particularly useful for filling in awkward gaps around decking and paving. Use them to cover electrical cables servicing outdoor lighting and pond pumps. The pool in the main picture has been made using contrasting swirls of coloured glass chippings laid in a shallow depression lined with butyl rubber sheeting. The planting around it consists of grasses and grass-like plants and is very stylised. You would not plant a pool like this – it is very much for show, and you would have

left: *Glass chippings have a space-age feel and look great combined with unusual foliage plants like these tufted grasses, as well as with plants having an architectural or sculpted feel. To work well, the surface must be kept clear of debris, so avoid glass chippings under deciduous trees. Combined with evergreen foliage plantings there are few problems. Glass chippings are laid in exactly the same way as decorative stone chippings or gravel. Prepare the ground for a hard surface by compacting the soil and adding a layer of hardcore. To ensure weed-free conditions, lay down a permeable landscaping fabric. This will also help to keep the glass chips clean. Periodically wash down the glass chippings with a hosepipe to keep them clean.*

to add an algicide in spring to stop the water from going green. A tiny submersible pump would keep the water moving, combating stagnation – you could replace the sculpted head with a waterspout.

Glass beads are more expensive and tend to be used in smaller quantities. They come in all colours, sometimes with an iridescent metallic coating. Use them as a decorative mulch for plant pots, to fill in awkward corners and to enhance self-contained water features.

Painting pots and planters

Skill level:

Painting or craft

experience useful

Best time to do:

Anytime

Special tools required:

Artist's paint brushes

and stencil brush

Time required:

An hour or two,

depending on the

number of coats of

paint required

WHAT YOU WILL NEED

• Clean pots in plastic, terracotta
or concrete
• Suitable paints, including
purpose designed pot paints,
artist's acrylics, coloured masonry
paints
• Brushes, natural sponge for
producing stippled or aged effects
• Sandpaper to roughen the
surface of shiny plastic pots
• Stencil, masking tape
• Paper to try out designs

You can now buy small pots of paint in earth tones or brighter shades specifically designed for painting terracotta and cement containers. Start with a clean dry pot and apply the paint according to the manufacturer's instructions. Plain painted pots can be used to enhance a particular colour scheme and a soft Mediterranean- or vivid Moroccan-blue contrasts well with orange, red, yellow or white and silver plantings. Ordinary artist's acrylic paints can also be used, though they might not last as long. Cover with a clear acrylic varnish, as extra protection, and line terracotta with plastic to prevent moisture seeping through and lifting the paint.

above: *Simple stripes transform a plain pot. Apply a base colour first and then paint the stripes using masking tape for guidelines.*

left: *You can really let your imagination run riot with hand-painted designs. But if you feel you need a little help, use a stencil.*

above: *It takes a degree of expertise to produce marbling of this quality. but in the garden you can get away with more rough and ready results. Practice your chosen technique on paper first and if you make a mistake on the pot, just paint over it. With practice, you will achieve results as good as these.*

Being plastic based, acrylic paints will also bond to plastic containers. When painting plastic, thoroughly scrub with detergent to remove any traces of grease, which will prevent the paint from sticking and on glossy surfaces, give the paint something to key onto by rubbing over with sandpaper. Textured masonry paints in neutral colours can be used on large plain plastic pots to great effect and these look well in a modern setting. For brighter shades use tubes of masonry paint colourisers. This kind of paint also bonds easily to concrete and terracotta.

Luxury detailing with metallics

Skill level:

Experience of

decorative paint effects

an advantage

Best time to do:

Any warm, dry spell to

encourage the paint

to dry quickly

Special tools required:

None

Time required:

Allow a day to paint a

large concrete object

WHAT YOU WILL NEED

• A reproduction stone effect
ornament
• Wire brush and scrubbing
brush
• Good quality paint brushes
• Knotting solution
• Metallic paint, strong
screwdriver to open tin and stir
contents
• Solvent to clean brushes
• Pair of thin latex gloves
• Newspaper to protect surfaces

In the garden, objects with a shiny metallic finish always attract attention – the contrast with natural materials and foliage is so great. The mirror like finish of modern metals such as chrome and polished stainless steel add a contemporary note, whilst brass fittings and fixtures suggest a nautical theme. The softer greys of zinc and aluminium blend in with any period or styling. But the one colour that will always stand out is gold. As well as giving the garden a feeling of luxury, *left: The mirror-like surface of this metal orb reflects distorted images of the garden. Raised on a pedestal, it appears symbolic, of magic and mystery! Chrome, polished stainless steel or silvering on glass will all produce this mirrored effect. But you could create a similar feel using a spherical concrete finial painted with hammer finish paint to suggest beaten metal or by covering the finial in gold leaf.*

below: This stone-effect finial could be treated in a variety of ways to increase its prominence. For example, the stone 'collar' could be painted gold and the sphere painted in a bright Moroccan blue, using masonry paint.

gold can also create a sense of fairytale magic and mystery. Use it sparingly for detailing – for example, to paint the ornamental tip of a metal obelisk or the odd leaf or flower in a blue or black wrought iron gate.

Few metallic paints are designed for use outdoors, and those that are tend to be for painting metalwork only. Bronze, copper and gold paints produce rich effects. Add a touch of opulence and glamour using these shades in plain or hammer finish to transform concrete urns and vases of classical styling or reproduction stone finials.

VARIATIONS ON THE THEME

Nothing creates the appearance of solid gold quite like gold leaf. Unfortunately expensive, it comes in very thin sheets that are applied with a brush.

below: This wind chime is decorated with a striking metallic sun motif and demonstrates how little touches of glittering metal can be used to good effect in the garden. You could paint a stone or terracotta wall plaque in a similar way or paint a wall mask or head planter in gold to hang half hidden on a climber-clad wall. Effects like this work especially well when the sun reflects off them.

Woven willow effects

Skill level:

Beginner gardener or

craft enthusiast. The

construction does not

have to be perfect!

Best time to do:

Anytime – depends on

when you can obtain

suitable materials

Special tools required:

None

Time required:

Allow one weekend

WHAT YOU WILL NEED

- Pre-soaked withies
- Wooden stakes
- Mallet to hammer the stakes
into the ground
- Secateurs to trim excess
- Clear exterior quality varnish
- Brush and brush cleaner

Woven willow and hazel structures create a rustic, country garden feel and can be the ideal finishing touch for a cottage garden. You might be able to cut your own fresh willow wands or withies in winter, but if not, you can always buy them from craft shops or mail order from basket makers in willow-growing regions. The withies will be dried and need to be soaked before use to make them pliable. Other materials can also be woven, including fresh bamboo stems taken from mature clumps and one-year-old growths from dogwoods like *Cornus alba*. Hard pruning every spring makes these plants produce long, straight unbranched stems, ideal for weaving.

The main picture shows a low woven fence used to emphasise the shape and pattern of the beds and to contain the planting within them. But you can also use pliable stems, such as bamboo, to

form a series of overlapping hoops that serve the same function. Push them into a lawn bordering a path or driveway as a signal not to tread on the grass.

To make a low fence such as the one illustrated, first hammer in a series of wooden pegs at intervals around the bed making sure that there is a peg at each corner or curve so that the weaving will follow the shape properly. Then, using one or two willow wands at a time, begin to weave them in and out of the pegs. Continue until the fence has reached the desired height.

below: The woven willow fence illustrated is quite easy to make and relatively inexpensive. You do not need any special equipment. Once the withies have been soaked, they are easy to manipulate and the fence builds quite quickly. To tidy it up, tuck all the stray ends in through the fence and trim right-angled corners using a pair of sharp secateurs. A construction of this kind should last around eight years, especially if it is coated with a clear exterior wood varnish, but it will weather pleasingly even if you leave it untreated. The only disadvantage to using fresh willow pushed into the ground in winter is that it is likely to sprout and take root, producing lush leafy growth. However, this may be fine for impromptu sculptures!

MAKING A WILLOW PERGOLA

A feature such as this can be grown quite quickly using willow because of its very fast growth rate. Here, four main plants have been grown straight then tied together at their tops so that they curve over. You may have to tie the stems to bamboo canes to get them to meet in the middle. All the side shoots have now been trimmed off, but to give the plants growing power, short side shoots will have been left in place during the training process. A latticework of stems has also been woven

at the back to form a kind of trellis. This would be best done with pre-cut withies, though you could plant a series of willow cuttings and train them up. They root very easily when pushed into damp ground. All that remains is to cut off any shoots that appear on the main uprights and to trim the profusion of leafy growth that forms the roof. Other suitable plants include lime, beech, hornbeam and laburnum.

Weaving and sculpting with ivy

Skill level:

Beginner gardener

Best time to do:

Late spring or early

summer, when plants

are growing strongly

Special tools required:

None

Time required:

A couple of hours

Ivy is an incredibly plastic and malleable plant that takes to being woven, and trained over frames with ease. Not only are the stems very flexible, they are also covered with leaves that act like little grappling hooks so that very little tying in is required. There are hundreds of different ivy cultivars and the many forms of English ivy, *Hedera helix*, are the ones to go for. Choose plants of different vigour and leaf size depending on the scale of feature you are trying to create. Some kinds are very vigorous and would quickly swamp a delicate topiary frame. Don't be tempted to use quick growing kinds for rapid results – they will not stop growing and you could find yourself constantly trimming to keep the shape under control. Also, avoid mixing different varieties, as these invariably have slightly different growth rates and one could take over. Plain green ivy with small leaves and short joints (distance between the leaves) are ideal for topiary, as the finished effect mimics traditional pieces clipped from box or yew. With heavily variegated ivy you do not see the shape as clearly. Ivy is self-clinging via little sucker pads, and can be used to soften a flight of steps or to decorate the base of a pedestal or stone ornament. It can also be used to create formal patterns on a plain wall. Trim the edge and face of the design a couple of times a year to keep it in bounds.

AN IVY ROPE PATH EDGING

An edging of ivy makes a neat way of outlining garden beds and borders or steps, giving them structure and winter interest. It is a novel alternative to a dwarf box or lavender hedge, and needs little clipping.

WHAT YOU WILL NEED

• Pots of rooted ivy cuttings, preferably with long trails. Choose all one variety to give even growth
• Stiff wire and wire cutters to make the hoop-shaped pins
• Scissors or secateurs to trim the ivy 'rope' when plaited

1 Plant ivies 45cm(18in) apart. Use all the same kind – either green or variegated varieties. Wait until the plants grow together and start to creep out onto the path before training them. No framework is needed.

2 Untangle the ivy trails, combing them with your fingers. Remove any dead, brown or damaged leaves to tidy the plants as you work. Lay out all the trails in roughly the same direction.

above: *You can train ivy and other trailing plants up a rustic wooden frame like this one. Alternatively, use a wire frame. The ivy will need occasional trimming.*

left: *A look of faded elegance! Keep the ivy under control so that the figure is not completely swamped. Slow-growing golden or heavily variegated ivy is ideal for decorating a statue in this manner.*

3 Beginning at one end of the row, gather up trails from either side and a strong one from the centre to plait together.

4 Work back along the row, tucking all the short shoots under the longer strands to hold them in place. Peg down the rope with some U-shaped hoops of stiff wire.

5 As the ivies grow the rope thickens out. You can either tuck the new shoots in amongst the mass of others or snip off the tips. This makes sideshoots develop from the main stems and thickens the rope.

Creating colourful backdrops

Skill level:

Beginner DIYer

Best time to do:

Any fine dry period

Special tools required:

None

Time required:

May take up to a

weekend

WHAT YOU WILL NEED

- Wire or nylon bristle hand brush
- Roller or paintbrushes depending on scale of job. A relatively small brush makes painting trellis easier
- Masonry paint for walls or microporous paints or coloured stains for woodwork
- Groundsheets to prevent splattering
- Gloves to protect hands

There is no doubt that the right colour of wall, fence or trellis can have a transforming effect on the garden. But before you start painting, it is as well to check with your local authority or estate office to see if there are any planning restrictions that might affect you. Only a few years ago it was very difficult to buy masonry paints in any colour other than white or a handful of neutral shades. That has all changed now, and colours include terracotta, Moroccan blue, and Mexican-style yellows and oranges. Be a little careful about what shade you choose. The relatively gentle light of northern latitudes tends to bring out blues most effectively and bright oranges, reds and yellows can seem out of place. Brilliant white walls can be too dazzling for sunny aspects but earth tones can make gentle backdrops for foliage and blend well with brighter blues. Before painting, brush down the brickwork or rendering with a wire brush, removing any loose paint flakes or crumbling mortar.

The range of paint colours and stains for wood has also exploded, and if you cannot find the exact shade you want, you can always blend colours from the same range. Always select proper exterior quality microporous paints that allow the wood to breathe and resist flaking. Blues, greys and soft greens work well in most situations and black is useful for adding a touch of drama in Oriental gardens. You might find that wood recently treated with preservative is difficult to colour and will need to be left to weather before paints and stains will take. Brush over with a nylon bristle hand brush and paint when the wood is absolutely dry. Use a roller or spray gun for quick coverage.

EASY-CARE TRELLIS If you nail trellis panels directly to a wall, it makes maintenance of the wall behind or the trellis itself very difficult. A better way is to fix the panels to wooden battens hinged at the bottom to allow access to the wall behind. Unscrew the hinges to remove the panels for painting.

above: *A soft yellow ochre covers this sunny wall and makes a cheerful backdrop for the potted citrus tree and blue chair. Use brighter colours sparingly.*

right: *Gentle blues really bring out the different shades of a flower border. This colour could also be used on trellis panels surrounding a Mediterranean-style terrace filled with terracotta pots.*

Transformations with paints and stains

Skill level:

Beginner gardener or

DIYer

Best time to do:

Any mild, dry spell

Special tools required:

None

Time required:

Depends on the size of

the project. An old

garden chair might take

a morning or afternoon

to prepare and paint

WHAT YOU WILL NEED

• Item of wooden furniture such
as an old bench or kitchen chair
• Sandpaper to rub down old
paintwork and remove splinters
• Microporous paint or stain or
exterior quality gloss paint –
useful for covering old chipped
paintwork
• Paintbrushes
• Brush cleaner
• Dustcloth or newspaper to
protect surfaces

Paints and stains can be used to highlight certain objects and structures in the garden. Use the same colour as a linking theme running through the garden. Colour can also be used to ease the transition between indoors and out with matching wood colours, pots and fabrics all helping to make the space feel connected and larger overall.

Often quite ordinary objects or ones no longer in use can be given a new lease of life with a lick of paint. Use special paints for metal objects such as watering cans and wrought iron furniture,

and microporous paints and stains for woodwork. Water based acrylic paints can be used to paint pots and ornaments of terracotta, concrete or plastic. Look out for old items of furniture and traditional gardening implements in junk shops and car boot sales, such as wheelbarrows and metal flower buckets. Even wicker baskets can be painted in different shades to fit a particular colour scheme.

above: *A green chair and blue bench seating add a splash of colour to this patio area. Unless you are going for a somewhat eccentric look or instead creating a children's play area, limit the number of colours used for furniture and woodwork to avoid clashes.*

VARIATIONS ON THE THEME

Making your own items of wooden furniture and garden structures creates all kinds of design possibilities. Paint is useful for hiding imperfections and helps protect against moisture ingress. Consider picking out the detail of structures like a trellis gazebo, perhaps using a darker shade to highlight the main struts and a paler shade to colour the trelliswork. An uninspiring garden shed could be given a similar treatment to transform it into a feature!

below: *This unusual bench table looks stunning painted in this powdery light blue colour. The paint not only picks up the colours of the plants in the border behind but also subtly reflects the bluey hue in the tiles that the bench table is standing on. The die-cut shapes in the table add to its decorative appeal and make it highly distinctive.*

Building garden seating

Mention garden seats and people think of either traditional wooden chairs and benches or lightweight portable garden furniture. Both can be surprisingly expensive to buy. Portable items have to be set up before use and then stored away under cover when they are no longer required, while traditional pieces (usually left outdoors in all weathers) are becoming an increasingly popular target for thieves. One inexpensive, permanent and thief-proof solution is to build your own seating

1 Build up the piers, positioning two bricks side by side and a third at right angles to them in each course. Check that each face is truly vertical.

2 Decide on the width of the bench and build up the second pier in the same way. Use a spirit level on a timber straightedge to check that the two piers are precisely level with each other. As an alternative to bricks you could use breezeblocks. Cover with fine chicken wire and apply a cement rendering.

3 Cut two support blocks from 50mm(2in) square softwood, slightly longer than the depth of the piers. Fix one to the outside of each pier with screws and wallplugs.

4 Cut two seat edge slats to length and attach them to the ends of the seat support blocks. The overlap at each end helps to conceal the support blocks.

left: *A classical style stone bench will weather over time and looks wonderful set into a flower border. It is a good idea to incorporate seating in this way.*

Round off the edges of the slats with sandpaper to prevent splinters.

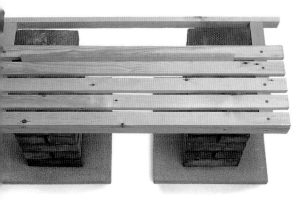

5 Screw on the first seat slat so that it rests on top of the front edge slat. Use a spacer slat to position the next one. Countersink all screw heads. Add more slats in the same way.

Bed support slabs on compacted subsoil and sand.

using bricks, mortar and preservative-treated wood. You can site a seat like this anywhere in the garden, but the best positions will allow you to catch the sun while you rest from your labours and admire the view. This simple bench consists of two piers of brickwork, built without the need for any cut bricks, and a slatted seat that is screwed unobtrusively to the masonry to create a sturdy, good-looking and surprisingly comfortable garden structure. You can build it directly on any existing paved or concrete surface; if you want to, site it down the garden, set on two paving slabs.

6 Apply two coats of clear preservative to keep rot and insect attack at bay, or use paint or stain if you prefer a coloured finish to the natural look.

Building a circular tree seat

No garden should be without some sort of seating, whether it is formal or informal. Gardeners deserve a rest from their labours from time to time, and visitors will appreciate the opportunity to sit and admire your handiwork. The type of seating you choose will depend on your taste and on the style of the garden. You may want to create simple bench seats in out-of-the-way corners; literally a plank of wood laid across two piles of bricks. Or you may decide to make the seating a major feature of your garden design like this circular tree seat. Whichever option you select, wood is the ideal material because it is so easy to work, warm and comfortable to sit on and dries off quickly after rain. However, durable hardwoods are expensive and cheaper softwood is prone to rot unless it has been treated with preservative and is well maintained. If you choose wood, you can build seating to your own plans or buy prefabricated benches and seats. The simpler styles – a plank on two posts, for example – are ideal for taking a short breather while you work. A seat can be as simple as a section of tree trunk or a large log on its side with a flat surface cut into it – perfect for the wild or woodland garden.

Masonry seats may be formed from paving slabs incorporated into raised planters and retaining walls, but stone is cold and retains moisture, so is best regarded as a summer seat surface. Keep some cushions to hand in the garden shed. Whatever type of seat you choose, position it carefully so that it forms an integral part of the garden design as well as providing a pleasant viewpoint.

WHAT YOU WILL NEED

- Prefabricated tree seat of the appropriate size
- Preservative paint or stain and brushes
- Shaped edging stones for the base
- Garden knife or trowel to cut round the turves
- Sand as a base for the stones
- Spanner to tighten the bolts

A TREE SEAT

A tree seat turns a bare tree trunk into an attractive garden feature that provides generous seating even in a small garden. Seats are available in various sizes to match a range of different tree diameters. Use curved moulded edging stones as a sturdy base for the legs and ensure all parts are level.

1 Buying a prefabricated tree seat avoids the need for fairly complex carpentry. Treat the seat with a preservative stain before assembling it.

2 Use curved moulded edging stones as a base for the legs of the seat. Lay them in position on the ground and cut carefully round them with a trowel.

3 Remove the turf. The ground will be hard and dry, so just lay a bed of sand. Put each moulded edging stone in place and tamp it down firmly to get it level.

4 Stand the first prefabricated seat section in place on its stones, then offer up the second section. Raise or lower the stones slightly as necessary to make everything properly level.

5 Thread the bolts through the predrilled holes. Add another washer before fitting the nut so that it does not bite into the wood. Tighten the bolts well.

6 Give the seat a new coat of preservative paint when necessary. Wood is ideal for garden use; it is both warm and comfortable to sit on and it dries off quickly after rain. Durable hardwoods are dearer than softwood but less prone to rot.

SIMPLE SEATS

Apart from rough and ready bench seats and stools, why not try a hammock? These are available from garden centres in summer and are easy to put up even if you don't have conveniently placed tree trunks! Hook one end onto a wall and hook the other from a short 10cm(4in) post set in concrete. Take care climbing in!

Garden illusions and effects with mirrors

Skill level:

Artistic skills and DIY

experience an

advantage

Best time to do:

Any period of fine, dry

weather

Special tools required:

None, but see list

below

Time required:

Allow a whole

weekend

WHAT YOU WILL NEED

• Suitable exterior paints for mural or stencilwork and clear exterior varnish
• Mirror (as alternative to a mural)
• Treillage panel
• Wall fixings and an electric drill and screwdriver
• Coloured micoporous paints or stains for woodwork, including a wooden archway or seating arbour such as the one illustrated

There are some effects, borrowed from the theatre, that can create depth in a garden and make a space feel much larger than it really is. They involve the use of murals, treillage panels that create false perspective and mirrors. A mirror mounted on a wall acts like a doorway, reflecting a view of the garden and giving the impression it is a way through to another area. It feels as though a bare wall, which before felt like a dead end and the boundary of the garden, has opened out into another area. The only problem with mirrors is that they can be hazardous to birds, which tend to fly into them, mistaking the reflected greenery for shrubs and trees. The problem is lessened by placing a piece of trellis over the mirror as illustrated in the picture to the right.

Bare rendered walls are perfect for painting directly onto. If you are reasonably skilled artistically you can paint your own garden scene freehand, creating a lush leafy backdrop to a patio or a landscape that takes the eye off into the distance.

above: *False perspective treillage panels can be great fun to use with mirrors especially in tiny high-walled courtyard gardens. Lush foreground planting is vital for the effect to work.*

left: *Paint murals freehand on a suitably prepared wall or use stencils of architectural detailing, potted plants, birds and insects. Paint stamps are easy to use and could create the effect of an ivy on a bare wall.*

above: *A perfectly executed* trompe l'oeil *at the end of a pathway uses steps, a trellis archway, potted plants and a mural to persuade the viewer that this is the entrance to a secret garden. The trug on the steps adds to the illusion.*

VARIATIONS ON THE THEME

To be really convincing, a trick of the eye or *trompe l'oeil* as they are better known, needs careful staging and positioning. Use foreground props like potted plants or a piece of statuary to create a sense of depth. Around a false doorway, build a trellis archway and smother it with climbers. You can even construct a shallow flight of steps to lead up to an opening as illustrated. Fix an old door onto the wall, use a mirror or paint a garden scene onto a wall – perhaps with a door ajar, leading into an imaginary landscape. An alternative to the doorway is the treillage walkway or corridor illusion, using false perspective panels positioned over a mirror. Foreground planting helps to conceal the extremities of the panels and strengthens the illusion overall. Seal mirrors using bituminastic paint and waterproof electrical tape.

Stone and ceramic spheres

Skill level:

DIY skills an advantage,

particularly experience

of mixing cement

Best time to do:

Anytime

Special tools required:

Strong craft knife

Time required:

One day

WHAT YOU WILL NEED

• Child's rigid plastic ball
• Strong craft knife
• Ready-mix cement and water
• Optional moss peat to make sphere weather more quickly
• Liquid detergent to act as plasticiser
• Wide plastic funnel to pour mix through hole in top of ball
• Optional masonry paint to colour cement ball when dry

An interesting development in recent years has been the appearance of more avant garde ornaments for the garden. Zen and minimalist influences have allowed very simply shaped abstract objects to become more acceptable and this has given far greater choice to the contemporary gardener.

One of these shapes is the sphere – always restful and calming to look at. At one end of the spectrum are the solid stone spheres which can be fabulously expensive, not to mention incredibly heavy. But they do weather beautifully. Then there are the terracotta spheres which are great for teaming up with terracotta pots or for contrasting with Moroccan blue paintwork. The biggest range is found in glazed ceramics with blue and teal green shades popular. Most are wonderfully mottled, and some have a slightly metallic iridescence. You can now also get ones with a kind of bronze metallic finish, as well as egg shapes and floating circular tablet shapes for the pool.

left: *This intriguing arrangement of solid stone spheres, an empty chair frame and a plain mirror creates a surreal atmosphere in this garden as well as a sense of space. Notice how the arc of the border and curving mowing stripes emphasise the circular themes and add further sculptural qualities. You can make your own stone effect spheres using cement, but you are limited to quite small globes. You can, however, achieve a similar weathered effect to that of stone by adding some moss peat to the cement mix. This organic element will encourage mosses and lichens to colonize. Another option is to wait until the cement is almost dry and score patterns in the surface, for example a wide spiralling line going from top to bottom.*

left: *Glazed ceramic spheres have a refreshing contemporary feel and look well set within a planted area where the contrasting textures and colours emphasise their smooth glossiness. Group in threes for greater impact.*

Spheres can look slightly odd if positioned singly, unless, as in the main picture, you are creating your own outdoor sculpture. Glazed ceramic spheres come in a range of sizes and look well clustered together in odd numbers amongst planting, next to a water feature or in a corner of the patio.

To make your own sphere, take a child's plastic ball and using a craft knife, cut a hole in one end large enough to pour in a cement mix. Make the mix fairly sloppy and add a few drops of liquid detergent as a plasticiser. Fill the mould and leave to set. Cut off the plastic.

Innovative garden lighting

Skill level:

Average DIYer, unless

doing electrical wiring,

in which case consider

calling in an electrician

Best time to do:

Fine weather for

candles, but electric

lights work anytime

Special tools required:

None

Time required:

Depends on project

WHAT YOU WILL NEED

• Selection of candles, flares, lanterns etc
• Ordinary clay plant pots as candle holders or glass jam jars to make your own lanterns
• Low voltage lighting kit for more permanent lighting and tools to install it
• White fairy lights for exterior use
• RCD or circuit breaker for safety

If you light up at least part of your garden at night, you will be able to enjoy those warm summer evenings to the full… Low voltage lights are easy to install and consist of a series of lamps on stalks or mini spotlights, running off a transformer; these are particularly useful for lighting the path leading to a front door, for example. However, if you have any doubt whatsoever about wiring up lights, seek a qualified electrician. The dangers of electricity are all the greater when you are installing lights and switches for outdoor use.

Uplighters at ground level can be angled to focus on a particular plant or the branches of a tree and strong architectural plants can really be made to look dramatic at night. Avoid flooding the whole garden with a security light – the effect is far from atmospheric and the light tends to cast

right: *A collection of outdoor lanterns and candle holders. This would suit a simple country or cottage garden setting or one slightly more contemporary. Take special care with candles.*

left: *This delightful scene shows how well candles can mingle with foliage and flowers to transform the night time garden. Notice how candles have been set at different heights in this corner of the garden to create a tiered effect. A good finishing touch for such a scenario might be a string of fairy lights hanging in the branches of the tree.*

huge, unattractive shadows around the garden. A pretty form of electric lighting includes tiny white fairy lights designed for outdoor use. Weave them through the climbers of an archway or pergola for a magical night time atmosphere.

If you want to create an air of luxury, consider outdoor candleholders and candelabras made of elaborate wirework or wrought iron and use heavy church candles in them, positioning them around the gvarden where they will illuminate shapely plants. Flares that stick in the borders around the patio are fun at barbeques and parties, as are candle lanterns hung from the trees or a pergola. Metal lanterns with a galvanized finish will not rust and look charming in most situations.

Index

Picture credits

The majority of the photographs featured in this book have been taken by Neil Sutherland and are © Salamander Books Ltd. The publishers wish to thank the following photographers for providing additional photographs, credited here by page number and position on the page, i.e. (B) Bottom, (T) Top, (C) Centre, (BL) Bottom left, etc.

Eric Crichton: Contents page (R second down, sixth down, seventh down), 7, 11(R), 22, 40(R), 45(TR), 46, 47(L), 47(R), 56(BL), 57, 59(R), 62(TL), 62–3(BL), 65(TR), 68, 70, 71(TR), 75(TR), 81(TR), 84(BR), 89(TR), 93(TR, BR), 96(B), 101(T), 103, 104(TR), 108(TL, B), 109, 122, 123(T, B), 124(TR), 137(L), 142, 143(TR), 148, 158(R), 162, 188(L), 196(B), 197, 205(TL), 211(BL), 214(TL), 216, 223(BL), 229(TR), 241(TL), 245(TL)
Garden Matters: 110(BR), 112(BR), 114(TL)

Garden Picture Library: 97, 113(R), 129(B), 218(T, B), 224(TR, BL), 225, 226, 227(TL), 228, 229(BR), 230, 236, 239, 244, 246, 247, 248, 249(TR)
John Glover: Contents page (R third down, fifth down), 16(BR), 32(BR), 35(TR), 51(TR), 53(TL), 54(BR), 61(TR), 62–3(C), 67(R), 72(CB), 73(TL), 86(L), 88, 91(TR), 96(TL), 99(BR), 101(B), 107(R), 111(R), 117(BL), 120(TL, BL), 121(R), 124(BL), 132–3(C), 133(R), 139, 141(TL), 145(TL), 147(T), 150(BL), 163(BL), 168–9(C), 169(R), 170, 189(TR), 190(L, BL), 191, 193, 194(TL,

BL), 195, 200, 213(TR), 215(R), 219, 222(BC), 231(BL)
Andrew Lawson: 64, 190(BR), 220(BL)
Clive Nichols: Title page, 6, 36, 76, 102, 113(TL), 115, 126, 129(T), 135(TL), 162 (designer Jean Goldberry), 182(TR), 237(R), 238
S&O Mathews: Contents page (BR), 10(TR), 12, 13(BL), 72(L), 125, 127, 128(BL), 130(BR), 136(C), 149(TL), 150(BR), 250
Harry Smith Collection: 87(TR)

Acknowledgements

Much of the material which makes up this book was previously published in *The Container Gardening Encyclopedia*, *The Practical Gardening Encyclopedia* and *The Encyclopedia of the Small Garden*. The publishers would like to thank all those who contributed to those publications and everyone involved in this book. See below for individual contributors.

Peter Blackburne-Maze, John Feltwell, Carol Gubler, Nicholas Hall, Ann James, Mike Lawrence, Colin Lewis, John Mattock, Jane Newdick, Sue Phillips, Yvonne Rees, Wilma Ritterhausen, Rosemary Titterington.

Thanks are also due to all those involved in the publication of the following titles in *The Practical Step-by-Step Guide* series: *Climbers and Trellis Plants*; *Container Gardening*; *Creative Garden Ideas*; *Garden Design*; *Garden*

Projects; *Growing & Displaying Roses*; *Growing Fuchsias*; *Growing Herbs*; *Growing Perennials*; *Heathers and Conifers*; *Patio Gardening*; *The Flower Garden*; *The Small Garden*.